Intel® Play™ QX3™ Computer Microscope

Lab Manual

PRENTICE HALL
Needham, Massachusetts
Upper Saddle River, New Jersey
Glenview, Illinois

Prentice Hall Science Explorer **Edition**

ISBN 0-13-068697-2
6 7 8 9 10 06

Intel® Play™ QX3™ Computer Microscope

Prentice Hall Science Explorer Edition

TABLE OF CONTENTS

INTRODUCTION

QX3 MICROSCOPE OPERATING INSTRUCTIONS

Intel® Play™ QX3™ Computer Microscope
Prentice Hall Science Explorer Edition

TABLE OF CONTENTS

LAB ACTIVITIES

TEACHER SUPPORT

INTRODUCTION TO THE QX3 MICROSCOPE

The Intel Play QX3 Computer Microscope School Edition allows your students to capture, magnify, and modify digital, microscopic, and macroscopic images. You can customize the use of the QX3 microscope to meet your curriculum needs by using activities in this guide and the included CD-ROM. The QX3 microscope permits innovative use of lab exercises designed around the Prentice Hall Science Explorer textbook series. With the QX3 computer microscope you can:

Magnify and View

Once the QX3 computer microscope is connected to a PC, the microscopic world can be explored like never before! Now you can:

- Place microscopic slides or specimens of all sizes under the QX3 computer microscope.
- Choose top or bottom lighting.
- Select from 10X, 60X, or 200X magnification.
- View incredible digital images!

Create and Combine

The software included with the QX3 computer microscope allows students to:

- Collect and save images.
- Modify images by adding text, changing video and audio effects—even add special effects!
- Create time-lapse movies to capture lab results.
- Produce videos and slide shows.

Share and Learn

Collaborative learning is promoted by:

- Printing images for use in reports and on stickers and posters.
- Sharing images with classmates on-screen.
- Sending images to classmates, teachers, and friends via email!

Everything you need to experience digital microscopy is included with Prentice Hall's School Edition QX3 Computer Microscope.

INTRODUCTION TO THE QX3 MICROSCOPE

Prentice Hall Science Explorer Lab Activities and the QX3

The lab activities in this guide are of two types: activities that correlate directly with the labs in the Prentice Hall Science Explorer texts and activities that extend the investigations found in the Prentice Hall Science Explorer series.

Direct Correlation Labs

These lab activities follow the format, set-up, and materials of existing Prentice Hall Science Explorer lab activities, while incorporating the use of the QX3 computer microscope where appropriate. In some activities, the use of the QX3 computer microscope replaces the use of a traditional compound light microscope or a hand lens in the activity. In other labs that did not originally use magnification of any sort, the activity is enhanced by the use of the QX3 microscope's capabilities.

Extension Labs

These lab activities follow the format and set-up of the Prentice Hall Science Explorer lab activities, but have some modifications to the activities that allow the QX3 microscope to be incorporated. For example, in some of the extension labs, the materials list has been modified to include examination of different types of items that make use of the QX3 computer microscope, while staying true to the focus and theme of the Prentice Hall Science Explorer activity.

Correlation Tables

The following tables list the Prentice Hall Science Explorer lab activities for Earth Science, Life Science, and Physical Science found in this guide. The tables provide the locations, lab types, and titles of each lab activity as found in the Science Explorer texts. In addition, the enhancements brought to these labs by the use of the QX3 microscope are listed here for quick reference. Each lab has also been assigned a Lab ID number for cross-referencing with the Master Materials List and Image Gallery List. Finally, all lab activities have been classified as either a direct correlation (DC) or extension (E) lab.

INTEGRATING THE QX3 MICROSCOPE WITH SCIENCE EXPLORER LABS

Prentice Hall Science Explorer, Life Science & Books A - E

Chapter (Page)	Lab Type	Lab Title	Using the QX3 Microscope Students Can...	Going Further Students Can...	Lab ID	Lab Type (DC/E)
LS 1 (p. 20) A 1 (p. 18)	**Try This**	**React!**	• Make movies that demonstrate pupillary response. • Make movies that demonstrate the blink reflex. • Capture macro images of external eye anatomy.	• Make a poster of the anatomical structures of the eye, labeled with their names and functions.	L1	E
LS 1 (p. 26) A 1 (p. 24)	**Skills Lab**	**Please Pass the Bread!**	• Capture images of different types of bread mold. • Make time-lapse movies of the growth of bread mold.	• Make a poster showing bread mold growth under different environmental growing conditions (bread with and without preservatives added).	L2	DC
LS 1 (p. 27) C 1 (p. 16)	**Discover**	**Is Seeing Believing?**	• Capture images of color and black and white newsprint. • Capture images of newspaper photographs.	• Compare microscopically photographs from a glossy magazine with those in newspapers.	L3	DC
LS 1 (p. 32) C 1 (p. 21)	**Sharpen Your Skills**	**Observing**	• Capture images of thin slices of cork and other specimens.	• Measure the size of the cork cells and estimate the number of cork cells in a cm^3.	L4	DC
LS 1 (p. 43) C 1 (p. 32)	**Skills Lab**	**A Magnified View of Life**	• Capture images of plant and animal cells. • Create a movie showing cyclosis in *elodea* cells.	• Observe their own skin or cheek cells.	L5	DC

INTEGRATING THE QX3 MICROSCOPE WITH SCIENCE EXPLORER LABS

Prentice Hall Science Explorer, Life Science & Books A - E

Chapter (Page)	Lab Type	Lab Title	Using the QX3 Microscope Students Can...	Going Further Students Can...	Lab ID	Lab Type (DC/E)
LS 2 (p. 80) C2 (p. 69)	**Skills Lab**	**Multiplying by Dividing**	• Capture images of the stages of mitosis in plant cells.	• Make a labeled poster illustrating the stages of mitosis. • Make a poster comparing mitosis in plants and animals.	L6	DC
LS 4 (p. 132) C 4 (p. 126)	**Discover**	**What Do Fingerprints Reveal?**	• Capture images of your own fingerprints and identify their characteristics.	• Create poster images that illustrate the three categories of human fingerprints.	L7	DC
LS 5 (p. 146) C 5 (p. 140)	**Discover**	**How Do Living Things Vary?**	• Capture images of very similar objects, such as sunflower seeds, to show their microscopic variation.	• Create poster showing different types of variation between organisms.	L8	DC
LS 7 (p. 222) A 3 (p. 84)	**Try This**	**Feeding *Paramecia***	• Make a movie of *Paramecium* feeding on algae.	• Make a time-lapse movie that shows how often *Paramecium* feeds each day.	L9	DC
LS 9 (p. 276) A 5 (p. 142)	**Try This**	**The In-Seed Story**	• Capture images of the parts of a seed, and label each part. • Measure the sizes of various seeds and seed parts.	• Create a poster showing the various sizes and different shapes of different seed types, with the appropriate labels.	L10	DC
LS 9 (p. 300) A 5 (p. 167)	**Skills Lab**	**Which Way Is Up?**	• Make a time-lapse movie of embryonic root growth in plants. • Make a time-lapse movie that illustrates the response of root growth to gravity.	• Design an experiment that tests your predictions about plants' growth responses to the sun—make a time-lapse movie of the experiment.	L11	DC

INTEGRATING THE QX3 MICROSCOPE WITH SCIENCE EXPLORER LABS

Prentice Hall Science Explorer, Life Science & Books A - E

Chapter (Page)	Lab Type	Lab Title	Using the QX3 Microscope Students Can...	Going Further Students Can...	Lab ID	Lab Type (DC/E)
LS 10 (p. 320) B 1 (p. 28)	**Discover**	**How Do Natural and Synthetic Sponges Compare?**	• Capture images of synthetic and real sponges for labeling and comparison.	• Make a poster showing the pore patterns in different types of real sponges, and compare these to a synthetic sponge.	L12	DC
LS 10 (p. 324) B 1 (p. 32)	**Try This**	**Hydra Doing?**	• Make a movie of locomotion in *Hydra.* • Make a movie of the feeding behavior of *Hydra.*	• Quantify the number of times *Hydra* will feed in a given length of time by making a time-lapse movie.	L13	DC
LS 13 (p. 410) B 4 (p. 120)	**Discover**	**What Are Feathers Like?**	• Capture images of different feather types and components.	• Make a poster of feather types from different birds, and make predictions about the lifestyle of each bird by the type of feathers examined.	L14	DC
LS 13 (p. 414) B 4 (p. 124)	**Skill Lab**	**Looking at an Owl's Leftovers**	• Create poster images of various prey animals from owl pellets.	• Create poster images of the skulls of various prey animals for use in prey identification.	L15	DC
LS 14 (p. 458) B 5 (p. 168)	**Real-World Lab**	**One for All**	• Make a movie of the daily activity of a portion of an ant colony. • Capture images of ant antomy.	• Make movies of ants feeding or drinking. • Capture images of different stages in the ant life cycle.	L16	DC

INTEGRATING THE QX3 MICROSCOPE WITH SCIENCE EXPLORER LABS

Prentice Hall Science Explorer, Life Science & Books A - E						
Chapter (Page)	**Lab Type**	**Lab Title**	**Using the QX3 Microscope Students Can...**	**Going Further Students Can...**	**Lab ID**	**Lab Type (DC/E)**
LS 15 (p.480) D 2 (p. 38)	**Discover**	**Hard as a Rock?**	• Capture images of the external surfaces of rocks and bones.	• Examine the internal structure of a broken bone. • Create a poster comparing the external and internal structure of bones. • Capture images of the external structure of a tooth (harder than bone).	L17	DC
LS 15 (p. 493) D 2 (p. 55)	**Skills Lab**	**A Look Beneath the Skin**	• Capture images of tendons, ligaments, muscles, and bones at the microscopic level.	• Create a poster showing the various components of a limb and their functions.	L18	DC
LS 15 (p. 494) D2 (p. 56)	**Discover**	**What Can You Observe About Skin?**	• Capture images of your own skin structure. Examine the effect of increased humidity on skin.	• Create a poster showing the various structures associated with skin (sweat pores, hairs, etc.) as well as pigmented/ non-pigmented areas.	L19	DC
LS 16 (p. 508) D 3 (p. 70)	**Sharpen Your Skills**	**Predicting the Presence of Starch**	• Capture images of starchy foods before and after the application of iodine. • Make a movie of the chemical reaction between starch and iodine.	• Create a poster showing the results of the starch test on different types of goods suspected of containing starch.	L20	DC

INTEGRATING THE QX3 MICROSCOPE WITH SCIENCE EXPLORER LABS

Prentice Hall Science Explorer, Life Science & Books A - E

Chapter (Page)	Lab Type	Lab Title	Using the QX3 Microscope Students Can...	Going Further Students Can...	Lab ID	Lab Type (DC/E)
LS 17 (p. 549) D 4 (p. 113)	**Discover**	**What Kinds of Cells are in Blood?**	• Capture images of the components of blood.	• Create a poster showing the different cell types in human blood, labeled with their names and functions.	L21	DC
LS 20 (p. 648) D 7 (p. 216)	**Real-World Lab**	**With Caffeine or Without?**	• Make a movie of the heart rate change in black-worms under different environmental conditions.	• Make a movie of heart rate changes in *Daphnia* in response to chemicals and/or temperature.	L22	DC
LS 23 (p. 737) E 2 (p. 65)	**Try This**	**Desert Survival**	• Capture images of the microscopic external and internal anatomy of a cactus.	• Create a poster illustrating the various structures found in a cactus along with a description of their function and their identity as a plant organ.	L23	DC
LS 23 (p. 746) E 2 (p. 74)	**Skills Lab**	**Change in a Tiny Community**	• Make a time-lapse movie of the organisms found in pond water to observe any changes in organism types over time.	• Design an experiment that would simulate the effect of changing seasons on the "pond." Make a movie of the effects of these changes as they occur.	L24	DC
LS 24 (p. 768) E 3 (p. 97)	**Discover**	**How Much Variety is There?**	• Capture images of different seed types	• Create a poster contrasting the seed diversity from a rainforest with that from a deciduous forest.	L25	DC

INTEGRATING THE QX3 MICROSCOPE WITH SCIENCE EXPLORER LABS

Prentice Hall Science Explorer, Earth Science & Books F - J

Chapter (Page)	Lab Type	Lab Title	Using the QX3 Microscope Students Can...	Going Further Students Can...	Lab ID	Lab Type (DC/E)
ES 1 (p. 9) H 1 (p. 30)	**Skills Lab**	**Speeding Up Evaporation**	• Make a time-lapse movie showing evaporation occurring.	• Make movies that explore evaporation rates under different experimental conditions.	E1	DC
ES 2 (p. 49) F 4 (p. 121)	**Sharpen Your Skills**	**Classifying**	• Capture images that illustrate color, crystal size, and luster in the minerals examined.	• Create a poster of the various minerals examined with labels describing their properties.	E2	DC
ES 2 (p. 53) F 4 (p. 125)	**Try This**	**Crystal Hands**	• Make a time-lapse movie of the growing of two different salt crystals—epsom salts and halite.	• Use polarized light to explore why sugar crystals glow and salt crystals do not glow.	E3	DC
ES 2 (p. 56) F 4 (p. 128)	**Discover**	**How Does the Rate of Cooling Affect Crystal Growth?**	• Make a movie of how cooling affects the crystal growth of salol.	• Make a poster showing the comparative salol crystals in response to various cooling rates. • Make movies that illustrate various crystal types based upon cooling rates.	E4	DC
ES 3 (p. 74) F 5 (p. 146)	**Discover**	**How Are Rocks Alike or Different?**	• Take snapshots of various kinds of thin sections of rocks. • View rock thin sections under polarized light by turning the QX3 microscope into a polarizing microscope.	• Create a poster that illustrates the mineral composition of various studied rock types.	E5	DC

INTEGRATING THE QX3 MICROSCOPE WITH SCIENCE EXPLORER LABS

Prentice Hall Science Explorer, Earth Science & Books F - J

Chapter (Page)	Lab Type	Lab Title	Using the QX3 Microscope Students Can...	Going Further Students Can...	Lab ID	Lab Type (DC/E)
ES 3 (p. 78) F 5 (p. 150)	**Discover**	**How do Igneous Rocks Form?**	• Capture images of rock types and make predictions about their formation based on their microscopic appearance.	• Create a poster of the various rock types, and label them with their methods of formation.	E6	DC
ES 3 (p. 84) F 5 (p. 156)	**Try This**	**Rock Absorber**	• Take snapshots to count the number of grains in course-grained rock samples.	• Create a poster that illustrates the difference between fine-grained and coarse-grain rocks.	E7	DC
ES 3 (p. 87) F 5 (p. 159)	**Discover**	**What Can You Conclude From the Way a Rock Reacts to Acid?**	• Capture images of the microscopic structure of limestone and coquina.	• Assemble a slide show of snapshots of calcite containing rocks, based on further experimentation.	E9	DC
ES 3 (p. 90) F 5 (p. 162)	**Discover**	**How do the Grain Patterns of Gneiss and Granite Compare?**	• Capture images of the grain structure in gneiss and granite.	• Create a poster that illustrates the relationship between gneiss and granite.	E8	DC
ES 6 (p. 183) F 3 (p. 93)	**Discover**	**What Are Volcanic Rocks Like?**	• Capture images of volcanic rocks.	• Create a poster that shows the features of volcanic rock compared to other types of rock.	E10	DC
ES 7 (p. 216) G 2 (p. 44)	**Try This**	**Rusting Away**	• Make a time-lapse movie of rust occurring on steel wool.	• Make a longer time-lapse movie that documents the ultimate fate of the steel wool pad.	E11	DC

INTEGRATING THE QX3 MICROSCOPE WITH SCIENCE EXPLORER LABS

Prentice Hall Science Explorer, Earth Science & Books F - J

Chapter (Page)	Lab Type	Lab Title	Using the QX3 Microscope Students Can...	Going Further Students Can...	Lab ID	Lab Type (DC/E)
ES 7 (p. 221) G 2 (p. 49)	**Discover**	**What is Soil?**	• Capture images of soil.	• Make a poster showing the particles making up soil.	E12	DC
ES 7 (p. 228) G 2 (p. 56)	**Real-World Lab**	**Getting to Know the Soil**	• Capture images of soil components.	• Make a slide show or poster illustrating the components of soil from different soil samples.	E13	DC
ES 8 (p. 275) G 3 (p. 94)	**Discover**	**What Can Be Learned from Beach Sand?**	• Capture images from beach sand showing the different components of the sand.	• Make a poster showing the components found in beach sand.	E14	DC
ES 9 (p. 286) G 4 (p. 106)	**Discover**	**What's in a Rock?**	• Capture images of the microscopic components of rocks.	• Create a poster of fossil remains in rocks.	E15	DC
ES 10 (p. 326) E 6 (p. 164)	**Discover**	**What's in a Piece of Coal?**	• Capture microscopic images of the structure and composition of coal.	• Create a poster comparing the structure of coal with fossil bearing rocks and coquina.	E16	DC
ES 11 (p. 368) H 2 (p. 53)	**Discover**	**What's in Pond Water?**	• Capture images of microlife forms found in pond water. • Make movies of micro-scopic life forms and their patterns of locomotion.	• Examine water from different ponds to create a poster illustrating the diversity of microlife in pond ecosystems.	E17	DC
ES 18 (p. 611) I 4 (p. 127)	**Try This**	**Modeling a Humid Climate**	• Make a time-lapse movie of humidity occurring within a covered bowl.	• Make a time-lapse movie of evaporative water loss in a warm "climate."	E18	DC
ES 18 (p. 618) I 4 (p. 134)	**Discover**	**What Story Can Tree Rings Tell?**	• Capture microscopic images of tree rings.	• Create poster images that measure and compare the growth of tree rings—creating a climate time line poster.	E19	DC

INTEGRATING THE QX3 MICROSCOPE WITH SCIENCE EXPLORER LABS

Prentice Hall Science Explorer, Physical Science & Books K - 0

Chapter (Page)	Lab Type	Lab Title	Using the QX3 Microscope Students Can...	Going Further Students Can...	Lab ID	Lab Type (DC/E)
PS 1 (p. 18) K 1 (p. 14)	**Discover**	**What Properties Help You Sort Matter?**	• Examine the microscopic features of different objects to help determine their properties.	• Create posters that show different ways of grouping items.	P1	DC
PS 3 (p. 91) K 3 (p. 89)	**Sharpen Your Skills**	**Observing**	• Make a time-lapse movie of zinc being dissolved from a penny core.	• Create a poster of images captured from time-lapse movie showing the penny before, during, and after the chemical reaction.	P2	DC
PS 4 (p. 118) L 2 (p. 63)	**Try This**	**Crystal Shapes**	• Examine the microscopic structure of various ionic compounds. • Capture images of different crystaline solids.	• Create a slide show that illustrates the crystal structures.	P3	DC
PS 4 (p. 120)	**Skills Lab**	**Shape Up!**	• Make a time-lapse movie of the evaporation of water from a salt solution. • Capture images of salt crystals produced before the experiment and during evaporation.	• Make a time-lapse movie of a similar procedure conducted on another ionic substance.	P4	DC
PS 4 (p. 128) L 2 (p. 72)	**Discover**	**How Small Do They Get?**	• Capture images of large and small salt crystals for comparison.	• Create a poster of the different sized salt crystals from this experiment, showing their similarity of structure.	P5	DC
PS 5 (p. 145) L 1 (p. 18)	**Try This**	**Mostly Cloudy**	• Make movies of a chemical reaction occurring.	• Quantify the length of time from start to completion of a chemical reaction.	P6	DC

INTEGRATING THE QX3 MICROSCOPE WITH SCIENCE EXPLORER LABS

Prentice Hall Science Explorer, Physical Science & Books K - O

Chapter (Page)	Lab Type	Lab Title	Using the QX3 Microscope Students Can...	Going Further Students Can...	Lab ID	Lab Type (DC/E)
PS 5 (p. 160) L 1 (p. 32)	**Discover**	**Can You Speed Up or Slow Down a Reaction?**	• Make movies of the reaction of vitamin C with iodine at different temperatures.	• Quantify the time necessary to complete a chemical reaction at various temperatures.	P7	DC
PS 6 (p. 178) L 3 (p. 80)	**Discover**	**What Makes a Mixture a Solution?**	• Examine the microscopic properties of different liquid mixtures.	• Design an experiment to determine what common liquid mixtures are solutions or suspensions. Students will make predictions first and then examine the mixtures microscopically to determine if the predictions were accurate.	P8	DC
PS 8 (p. 250) L 4 (p. 118)	**Sharpen Your Skills**	**Classifying**	• Capture images of natural and synthetic fibers.	• Make a poster showing the key differences between natural and synthetic fibers.	P9	E
PS 8 (p. 252) L 4 (p. 120)	**Real-World Lab**	**Packaging with Polymers**	• Investigate the microscopic properties of different polymers.	• Create a poster that relates the microscopic structure of each polymer with its performance as a packing material.	P10	DC
PS 8 (p. 255) L 4 (p. 123)	**Discover**	**Are They Steel the Same?**	• Capture images of corroded surfaces.	• Create a poster that shows corrosion on steel treated in different manners.	P11	DC
PS 8 (p. 260) L 4 (p. 128)	**Discover**	**Does it Get Wet?**	• Capture images of porous and nonporous containers.	• Make a poster illustrating the microscopic differences between glazed and unglazed pottery.	P12	DC

INTEGRATING THE QX3 MICROSCOPE WITH SCIENCE EXPLORER LABS

Prentice Hall Science Explorer, Physical Science & Books K - O

Chapter (Page)	Lab Type	Lab Title	Using the QX3 Microscope Students Can...	Going Further Students Can...	Lab ID	Lab Type (DC/E)
PS 9 (p. 296) M 1 (p. 28)	**Discover**	**How Slow Can it Flow?**	• Make a time-lapse movie of the movement of honey, molasses, or corn syrup, so that they can quantify the velocity of the fluid.	• Make and test predictions about what conditions could alter the velocity of the fluid.	P13	DC
PS 10 (p. 330) M 2 (p. 62)	**Real-World Lab**	**Sticky Sneakers**	• Capture images of magnified views of various surfaces to understand how they can impact friction. • Create poster images that illustrate experimental results.	• Create poster images that provide an increasingly magnified perspective on whether "a smooth surface is really smooth."	P14	DC
PS 17 (p. 536) O 3 (p.78)	**Try This**	**How Do Light Beams Behave?**	• Visualize the principle behind polarizing filters.	• Make a movie showing the effect of using cross-polarized filters on the transmission of light.	P15	E
PS 22 (p. 718) N 4 (p. 120)	**Discover**	**Are You Seeing Spots?**	• Capture images of a computer monitor screen at various magnifications.	• Make a poster showing how a television or computer monitor makes an image using small dots of color.	P16	DC

LAB CORRELATION TO NSES

National Science Education Standards (NSES) Correlation

National Science Education Standards	Life Science Labs	Earth Science Labs	Physical Science Labs
CONTENT STANDARD A: SCIENCE AS INQUIRY			
A-1 Identify questions that can be answered through scientific investigations.	L1-L25	E1-E19	P1-P16
A-2 Design and conduct a scientific investigation.	L9,L11,L22,L24	E3, E9, E18	P4, P11, P13
A-3 Use appropriate tools and techniques to gather, analyze, and interpret data.	L1-L25	E1-E19	P1-P16
A-4 Develop descriptions, explanations, predictions, and models using evidence.	L1-L25	E1-E19	P1-P16
A-5 Think critically and logically to make the relationships between evidence and explanations.	L1-L25	E1-E19	P1-P16
A-6 Recognize and analyze alternative explanations and predictions.	L2, L11, L14, L20, L22, L24	E3, E4, E9	P4, P6, P7, P8, P13
A-7 Communicate scientific procedures and explanations.	L1-L25	E1-E19	P1-P16
A-8 Use mathematics in all aspects of scientific inquiry.	L4, L9, L13, L22	E1, E11, E18, E19	P6, P7, P13

LAB CORRELATION TO NSES

National Science Education Standards (NSES) Correlation

National Science Education Standards	Life Science Labs	Earth Science Labs	Physical Science Labs
CONTENT STANDARD B: PHYSICAL SCIENCE			
B-1 Properties and changes of properties in matter.	—	—	P1, P2, P3, P4, P5, P6, P7, P8, P9, P10, P11, P12
B-2 Motions and forces.	—	—	P13, P14
B-3 Transfer of energy.	—	—	P6, P7, P15, P16
CONTENT STANDARD C: LIFE SCIENCE			
C-1 Structure and function in living systems.	L1, L4, L5, L6, L7, L10, L12, L13, L14, L17, L18, L19, L23	—	—
C-2 Reproduction and heredity.	L2, L6, L8	—	—
C-3 Regulation and behavior.	L1, L9, L10, L11, L13, L16, L24	—	—
C-4 Populations and ecosystems.	L8, L15, L16, L23, L24	—	—
C-5 Diversity and adaptations of organisms.	L2, L8, L12, L15, L16, L25	—	—
CONTENT STANDARD D: EARTH AND SPACE SCIENCE			
D-1 Structure of the Earth system.	—	E2, E5, E6, E7, E8, E9, E10, E12, E14	—
D-2 Earth's history.	—	E9, E10, E14, E15, E16, E17, E19	—
D-3 Earth in the Solar System.	—	—	—

LAB CORRELATION TO NSES

National Science Education Standards (NSES) Correlation

National Science Education Standards	Life Science Labs	Earth Science Labs	Physical Science Labs
CONTENT STANDARD E: SCIENCE AND TECHNOLOGY			
E-1 Abilities of technological design.	L1-L25	E1-E19	P1-P16
E-2 Understandings about science and technology.	L1-L25	E1-E19	P1-P16
CONTENT STANDARD F: SCIENCE IN PERSONAL AND SOCIAL PERSPECTIVES			
F-1 Personal health.	L18, L19, L20, L22	—	—
F-2 Populations, resources, and environments.	L8, L9, L15, L16, L23, L24, L25	E1, E13, E14, E17, E18, E19	—
F-3 Natural hazards.	—	E10, E17, E18, E19	—
F-4 Risks and benefits.	—	—	—
F-5 Science and technology in society.	—	—	—
CONTENT STANDARD G: HISTORY AND NATURE OF SCIENCE			
G-1 Science as a human endeavor.	L1-L25	E1-E19	P1-P16
G-2 Nature of science.	L1-L25	E1-E19	P1-P16
G-3 History of science.	L4, L6	E7	P9

IMAGE CORRELATION

The following curriculum-based images are included on the QX3 Operating Software. The table below correlates them to the lab activities in this manual, as well as to the Science Explorer Textbook chapters for Life Science, Earth Science and Physical Science.

Image	Lab ID	Life Science Chapter	Earth Science Chapter	Physical Science Chapter
Amphipod	E17, L24	12	-	-
Animal Mitosis Search	L6	2	-	-
Asian Lady Beetle	L16	12, 22	-	-
Bacteria as Food	-	6	-	-
Beach Sand Sort	E14, E15, E16	-	7	-
Bean Seed	L8, L10	9	-	-
Bee	L16	12	-	-
Blood Cells	L21	17	-	-
Blood Parasite	L21	12, 22	-	-
Bone-forming Tissue	L17	15	-	-
Bread mold (*Rhizopus*)	L2	7	-	-
Capillary	L12	17	-	-
Cardiac Muscle	L18	15, 17	-	-
Cat Hair	-	13	-	-
Cells in a Tissue	L18	15	-	-
Cells in an Organ	L18	15	-	-
Chick Embryo 72 hours	-	13, 21	-	-
Chloroplasts	L5	1, 2, 9	-	-
Citrus Mold (*Penicillium*)	L2	7	-	-
Colon Interior	L18	16	-	-
Colon Polyp	L18	16	-	-
Color-shifting Ink	-	-	18	
Common Mineral	E2	-	2	-
Construction Mineral	E2	-	2	-
Copepod	E17, L24	12	14	-
Cork Cells	L4	1	-	-
Corn Earworm	L16	12	-	-
Corn Leaf	-	9	-	-
Cotton Boll Weevil	L16	12	-	-
Cotton Boll Worm	L16	12	-	-
Crossed Threads	L3, P9	-	-	-
Crystal	E2, E3, E4, P4, P5	-	2	17
Crystal Group	E2, E3, E4, P4, P5	-	2	-
Cyanobacteria	-	6	-	-
Daphnia	E17, L24	12	-	-

Intel® Play™ QX3™ Computer Microscope

Prentice Hall Science Explorer Edition

IMAGE CORRELATION

Image	Lab ID	Life Science Chapter	Earth Science Chapter	Physical Science Chapter
Desmid	E17, L2	4,7	-	-
Developing Pine Cone	L10	9	-	-
Diatoms	E17, L24	7	14	-
Double Refraction	P15	-	2, 3	15
Down Syndrome	-	4	-	-
Earthworms	L22	10	-	-
Eye Interior	L1	20	-	-
Fabric Weave	L3	-	-	-
Feather	L14	13	-	-
Feeding Mite	L16	12	-	-
Feldspar	E2	-	2, 3	-
Fern Spore Case	L10	8	-	-
Fingerprint	L7	-	-	-
Fire Ants	L16	12	-	-
Fire Rock	E5, E6, E7, E8, E10	-	3, 6	-
Flea	L16	12, 22	-	-
Flesh-eating Larva	L16	12	-	-
Flower	-	9	-	-
Flower Anatomy	-	9	-	-
Flower Pollinator	L16	9, 12	-	-
Fluorescent Minerals	E2, P15	-	2	-
Fluorite	E2	-	2	-
Forest Fungi	-	7	-	-
Fruit	-	9	-	-
Fungal Hyphae	-	7	-	-
Fungus Gills	-	7	-	-
Generalized Animal Cell	L4	1	-	-
Generalized Plant Cell	L4	1	-	-
Geode	E2, E3, E4, P4, P5	-	2, 3	-
Glassy Luster	E6, E10	-	2	-
Gold	E2	-	2	-
Gram Stain Reaction	-	6	-	-
Gypsy Moth Predator	L16	12	-	-
Head Louse Adult	L16	12	-	-
Head Louse Nit	L16	12	-	-
Head Louse Nymph	L16	12	-	-
Herbaceous Stem	-	9	-	-
Hessian Fly	L16	12	-	-
Honey Bee Brood Cell	L16	12	-	-

Intel® Play™ QX3™ Computer Microscope
Prentice Hall Science Explorer Edition
IMAGE CORRELATION

Image	Lab ID	Life Science Chapter	Earth Science Chapter	Physical Science Chapter
Hookworm	-	10, 22	-	-
Human Chromosomes	L6	3	-	-
Human Hair	-	13	-	-
Hydra	L13	10	-	-
Insect Antennae	L16	12	-	-
Insect Cornea	L16	12	-	-
Insect in Amber	E15, E16, L16	12	9	-
Insect Predator	L16	12	-	-
Insect Wings	L16	12	-	-
Intestine Tissue	L18	16	-	-
Jewelry Mineral	E2	-	2	-
Lady Beetles	L16	12, 23	-	-
Ladybugs	L16	12, 23	-	-
Laying an Egg	L16	12	-	-
Leaf-cutting Ant	L16	12	-	-
Leaf Edge	-	9	-	-
Lichen	-	8	-	-
Light through Sillimanite Rock	P15	-	3	17
Liver Fluke	-	10, 22	-	-
Liver Tissue	L18	16	-	-
Lung Tissue	L18	18	-	-
Lyme Tick Adult	L16	12	-	-
Lyme Tick Nymph	L16	12	-	-
Mammoth Tooth E	15, E16	-	9	-
Man-made Bismuth	E2	-	2	-
Man-made Quartz	E2, E3, E4, P4, P5	-	2	-
Maple Black Spot	L2	7	-	-
Maple Leaf	-	9	-	-
Marble	E2	-	3	-
Metal Ore	E2	-	2	-
Microdot Printing	-	1	-	-
Mineral Color	E2	-	2	-
Mineral Hunt	E2	-	2	-
Minerals are Useful	E2	-	2	-
Mite	L16	12	-	-
Molds	L2	7	-	-
Mosquito Feeding	L16	12	-	-
Mosquito Wriggler	L16	12	-	-

Intel® Play™ QX3™ Computer Microscope
Prentice Hall Science Explorer Edition

IMAGE CORRELATION

Image	Lab ID	Life Science Chapter	Earth Science Chapter	Physical Science Chapter
Mouth Bacteria	-	6	-	-
Mud Bee	L16	12	-	-
Musk Ox Jaw	E15, E16	13	9	-
Natural Fiber	P9	-	-	-
Nature's Concrete	E6, E9, E15, E16	-	3	-
Nerve Cells	L18	20	-	-
Newsprint	L3	1	-	-
Normal Female Karyotype	-	4	-	-
Normal Male Karyotype	-	4	-	-
Oil-Degrading Bacteria	-	6	14	-
Orb Spider	L16	12	-	-
Oscillatoria	E17, L2	4,6	-	-
Paper Fibers	L2	-	7	-
Paramecium Crystals	L9, P15	7	-	-
Peach Pit	L10	9	-	-
Petrified Wood	E19	5	9	-
Pipes and Wires	E2	-	2	-
Planaria	E17, L24	10	-	-
Plant Mitotic Search	L6	2	-	-
Polarized Light through Sillimanite	P15	-	-	17
Pollen	L10	9	15	-
Pollinating a Flower	L16	9, 12	-	-
Pond Scum	E17, L24	7	-	-
Pore Mushroom	-	7	-	-
Potato Beetle	L16	12	-	-
Prokaryotic and Eukaryotic Cells	L4	1	-	-
Pumice	E10	-	3, 6	-
Rod-Shaped Bacteria	-	6	-	-
Root Hairs	-	9	-	-
Root Nodule Bacteria	-	23	-	-
Rust	E11, P11	-	2	3
Sac Fungus	-	7	-	-
Sawfly Adult	L16	12	-	-
Sawfly Larvae	L16	12	-	-
Scaly Leaves	L25	9	-	-
Scar Tissue	L18	15	-	-
Sipping Nectar	L16	9, 12	-	-

Intel® Play™ QX3™ Computer Microscope

Prentice Hall Science Explorer Edition

IMAGE CORRELATION

Image	Lab ID	Life Science Chapter	Earth Science Chapter	Physical Science Chapter
Skeletal Muscle	L18	15	-	-
Smooth Muscle	L18	15	-	-
Soil Root	-	9	-	-
Sphere Bacteria	-	6	-	-
Spirogyra	E17, L24	7	-	-
Square Minerals	E2	-	2	4
Starch Grains	L20	2, 16	-	-
Starfish	-	11	-	-
Strawberry	-	9	-	-
Streak	E2	-	2	-
Sugar Glow	P15	-	-	17
Sulfur	E2	-	2	4
Summer Eggs	L24	12	-	-
Synthetic Fiber	P9	-	-	-
Table Salt	E2, E3, E4, P4, P5	-	2	4
Tapeworm	-	10	-	-
Tarnished Plant Bug	L16	12	-	-
Termite Nest	L16	12	-	-
Termite Swarmers	L16	12	-	-
Thread Algae	E17, L24	7	-	-
Toothpaste	E2	-	-	-
Trillium	-	9	-	-
Volcanic Glass	E6, E10	-	3, 6	-
Volvox	E5, E6, E8, E17, L24	7	-	-
Wasp	L16	12	-	-
Water Leaf	-	9	-	-
Water Softener	P4	-	2, 3	-
Wood Rings	E19	9	18	-
Wood Rot	-	7	-	-
Woody Stem	-	9	-	-
Yeast Cells	-	2, 7	-	-

Intel® Play™ QX3™ Computer Microscope
Prentice Hall Science Explorer Edition

OPERATING INSTRUCTIONS

Minimum System Requirements

- A computer that is USB enabled (Most computers manufactured after June 1998 are USB enabled.)
- Microsoft® Windows® 98, Intel® Pentium® or Celeron™ processor 200 MHz or faster (or equivalent)
- 32 MB of RAM
- Minimum 150 MB hard disk space
- Quad speed (4x) CD-ROM
- 800x600 display, 16-bit color
- Windows compatible sound device
- Video and sound compatible with DirectX®

Package Contents

Check the contents of your package. You should have all the items listed below. If anything is missing or damaged, contact Neo/SCI Technical Assistance at 1-800-526-6689 or at **http://www.neosci.com.**

- Intel Play QX3 Computer Microscope (microscope with USB cable and stand)
- Operating software (CD-ROM) with image gallery
- This curriculum guide and a registration card
- A coupon from Neo/SCI Corporation to purchase additional computer microscopes at a discount.

Safety Information

Using the QX3 microscope safely:

- When setting up the work area, make sure that the monitor can be easily viewed while placing specimens on the sample platform.
- Demonstrate the safe reach of the USB cable.
- Encourage responsible use and care of the equipment.
- Be especially careful when using liquids around electrical equipment.
- Only an adult should change the microscope bulbs and replace the lens cover (if necessary).
- If you use an additional light with your microscope, do not use a lamp with a halogen or other high-heat bulb that could cause burns if accidentally touched.
- Upper and lower illumination surfaces can get very warm.

OPERATING INSTRUCTIONS

Care and Maintenance/Replacement Parts Information

Replacement bulbs and lens covers may be ordered by contacting Neo/SCI Technical Assistance at 1-800-526-6689 or at **http://www.neosci.com.**

Cleaning the sample platform:
The sample platform should be wiped clean with a damp cloth after each use. The stand and microscope should also be wiped clean whenever required.

Caring for the lens cover:
The protective lens cover on the QX3 microscope may become dirty with use. Use only canned air to clean it. Never use a lens brush or other rubbing method to clean the lens cover. Avoid the use of liquid cleaners.

Lens cover replacement:
If the lens cover becomes severely smudged, scratched, or stained, it should be replaced.

1. The cover is replaced by removing the two Phillips head screws and discarding the damaged cover.
2. Secure the replacement cover with the retained Phillips head screws. Do not over-tighten.

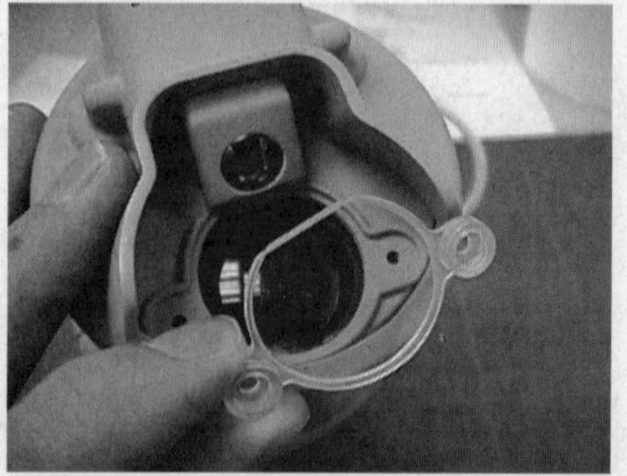

Changing bulbs:
Bulbs used in the QX3 microscope are a special type not found in stores. Replacement bulbs other than authorized Intel Play bulbs may cause damage to your microscope and void your warranty. Replace a bulb whenever there is a noticeable decrease in light output. Adequate light is needed to get the best capture with the microscope.

IMPORTANT: *The bulbs become hot when operating. Make sure the bulb has fully cooled to room temperature before replacing. Do not touch the surface of the replacement bulb with your fingers. Use a cloth or cotton glove to prevent damage to the bulb.*

To change bulbs, follow these steps:

Upper bulb replacement

1. Unplug the USB cable from your computer.
2. Remove the microscope from the base.
3. Remove the single screw holding the bulb retainer in the microscope housing.
4. Remove and discard the old bulb.
5. Insert the new bulb, replace the bulb retainer, and reattach the USB cable.

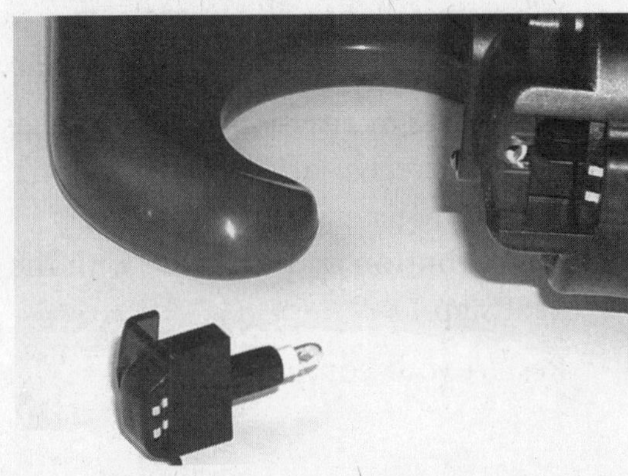

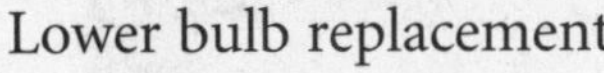

Lower bulb replacement

1. Unplug the USB cable from your computer.
2. Remove the microscope from the base and set it aside.
3. Remove the bulb cover on the bottom of the sample platform by loosening two screws.

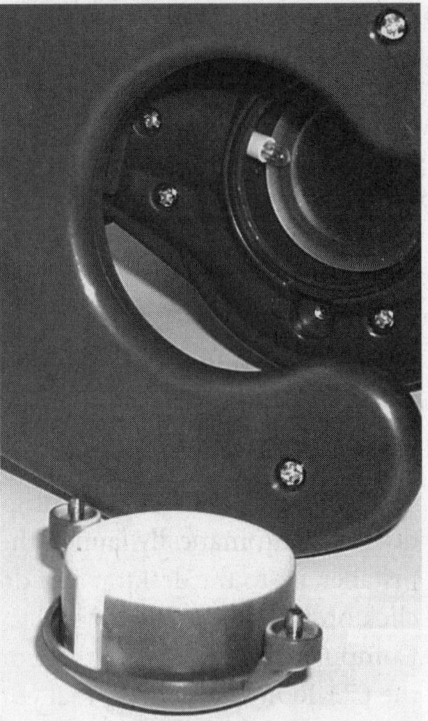

4. Remove and discard the old bulb.
5. Insert the new bulb, replace the bulb cover, and reattach the USB cable.

Audio help function:

Click on the Help button to use the software's Audio Help. The cursor changes to a question mark (?). Pause over items and you will hear their names and how to use them.

Intel® Play™ QX3™ Computer Microscope
Prentice Hall Science Explorer Edition

PRENTICE HALL SCIENCE EXPLORER

OPERATING INSTRUCTIONS

Setup Guide

Software installation:
STOP! *Do not attach the microscope to your computer! It is important that you install the software first. Here's how to install the QX3 software:*

- Insert the Intel Play QX3 Computer Microscope CD.
- Wait for the Autoplay to start.
- Click the Install button. (If Autoplay does not automatically launch the installer, go to the desktop and double-click on the icon named "My Computer." Double-click the icon for the CD-ROM/DVD drive that contains the QX3 software. Sometimes this will cause Autoplay to start. If it doesn't, open the setup folder, double-click on setup.exe, and follow the setup steps on this page.)
- Follow the steps by clicking the appropriate buttons.

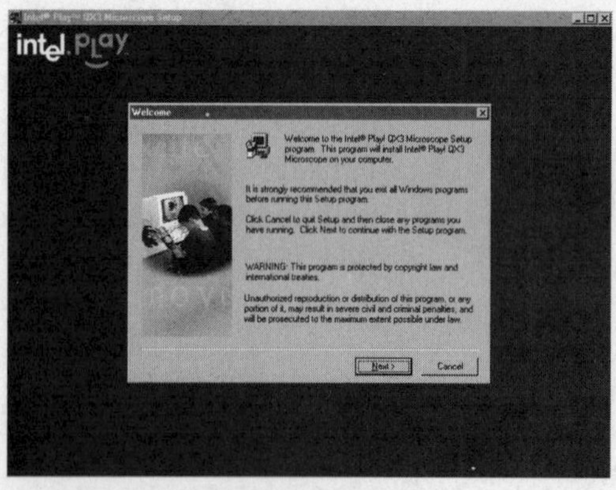

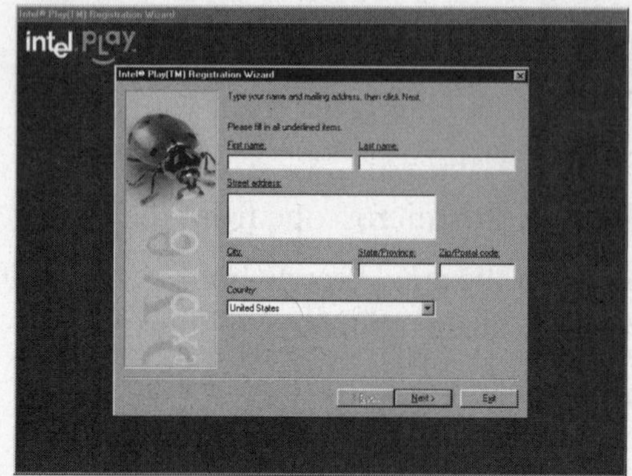

- When installation is complete, you can register your QX3 microscope online.
- Follow the instructions on the e-registration screens. (If you can't or don't want to register online, click the Cancel button and continue with the next step.)
- Restart your computer.

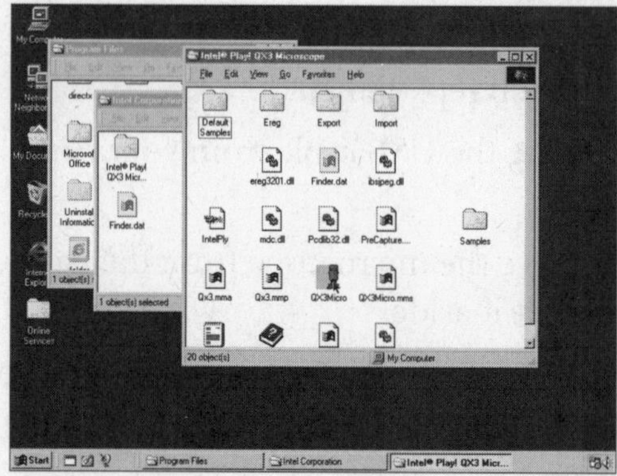

- Once the Windows desktop appears, plug the microscope cable into your computer's USB port.
- Now that you have plugged in your microscope, double-click on the QX3 icon to launch the software. You can also launch the software by using the Windows Start menu.

Intel® Play™ QX3™ Computer Microscope
Prentice Hall Science Explorer Edition

OPERATING INSTRUCTIONS

IMPORTANT: *Make sure to check the Read Me file for any tips or important information written since this guide was printed. To access the Read Me from your Windows Start menu, click Start, point to Programs, point to Intel Play QX3 Microscope and then click QX3 Read Me.*

- If you have any problems with the setup procedure, first make sure you have followed these instructions exactly. If you did, please do the following:
- Unplug the USB cable.
- Restart your computer.
- Repeat the setup steps.
- If you are still having problems, see the Troubleshooting section of this guide.

Uninstalling the QX3 software:
To uninstall your QX3 software from the Windows Start menu, click Start, point to Programs, point to Intel Play QX3 Microscope, and then click Uninstall QX3 Microscope. To reinstall the software, see the Setup Guide section, or press F1 for Online Help.

Remember this—

- If disk space is limited, urge your students to delete unwanted captures when they finish playing.
- Alt-F4 is a function of Microsoft Windows that will quit an application. Also Alt-Tab will cycle through open applications. Remind your students to avoid these keystrokes when using the QX3 software.

Using the Intel Play QX3 Computer Microscope Controls

The QX3 microscope consists of a base stand and a detachable microscope. There are two light sources: one in the sample platform and another in the microscope.

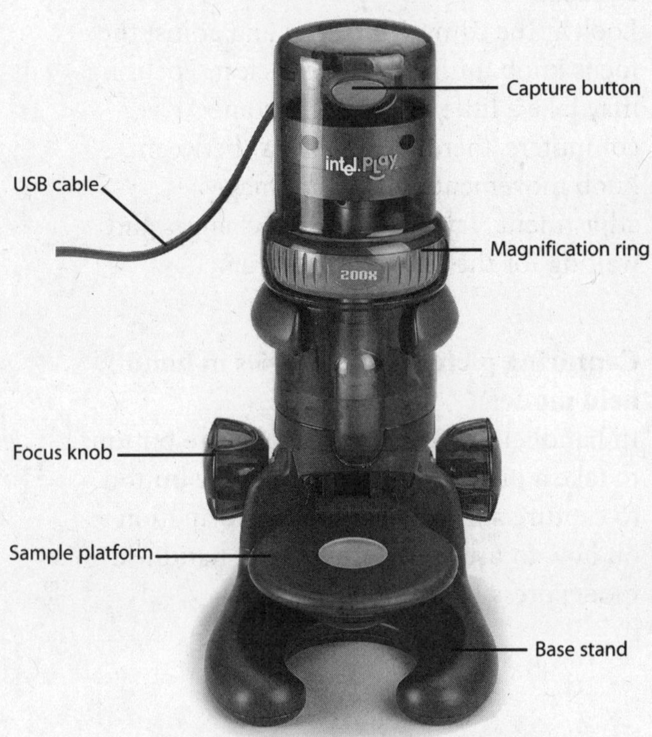

The base also has focus knobs, and the microscope has a magnification ring and Capture button. Once the software is running, you can use the controls on the microscope to focus, change magnification level, and capture pictures or movies (in handheld mode).

Changing magnification:
Choose the level by rotating the magnification ring on the microscope until the desired magnification level label faces you. You will hear a click when the lens is properly aligned.

The levels correspond roughly to 10X, 60X, and 200X. These magnification levels are approximate and have been measured using a 15 in. (38 cm) monitor. Actual magnification will vary according to the size of your monitor.

Focus:
Look at the computer screen and adjust the focus knob until the image is clear. Focusing may take a little practice. On some computers, there can be a delay between knob movement and screen image adjustment. Try making small changes and waiting for the screen to catch up.

Capturing pictures and movies in hand-held mode:
In handheld mode, click the Capture button to take a picture. Click and hold the button to capture a movie. For more information on how to use the microscope in handheld mode, press F1 for Online Help.

NOTE: *In handheld mode, focus by slowly moving the microscope closer to or farther away from the object being examined. You can get a good idea of the focal range with the microscope on the base stand and watching the upper and lower limits of the focus adjustment.*

Software Notes

Button basics:
Use the software by clicking on buttons and using tools. You will see different buttons on different screens.

Live View button
Go to Live View from Main to view and add samples to your collection.

Main button
Go to Main, which lets you choose fun things to do with your pictures and movies.

Intel® Play™ QX3™ Computer Microscope
Prentice Hall Science Explorer Edition

OPERATING INSTRUCTIONS

OK button
Continue your action. This button usually appears with the Cancel button.

Cancel button
Cancel your action. This button usually appears when you enter special screens, like the show editing window and when you quit the software.

Quit button
Quit the QX3 software. You need to go to Main to quit.

Lighting

The QX3 lights are controlled by the software. The microscope lights turn on automatically when you enter Live View. They turn off when you go to Main, where they are not needed.

Lighting controls
You control the lights in Live View with the Lighting Controls on the screen. Click the top bulb to use top lighting. Click the bottom bulb to shine light up through the sample platform. Moving the slider up makes your sample look brighter. Moving it down makes your sample less bright. Experiment to find what works best with your samples. When you remove the microscope from the base, the top light comes on automatically.

Using the right light
Use the bottom light to shine light up through transparent and very thin samples (e.g., feathers, slices of vegetables, onion skin). The light in the detachable microscope illuminates objects that are too large or heavy to be placed on the microscope's sample platform. You can also use the microscope on the stand to view small solid objects and living specimens with top lighting.

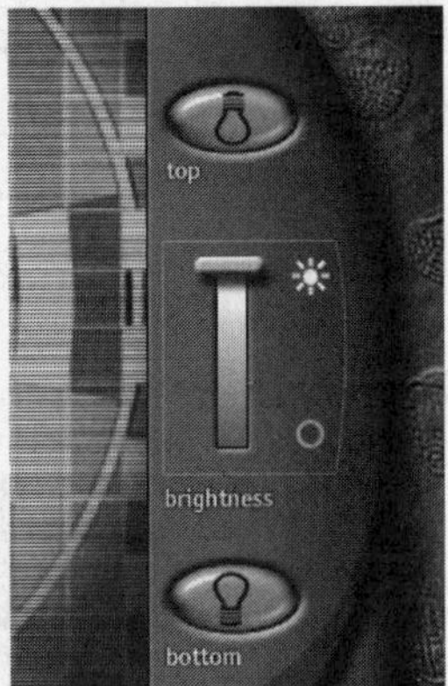

Adding extra lighting
Ordinary household light works fine with the QX3 microscope. You may want to place a high-intensity desk lamp near the microscope to add to top lighting when using medium or high magnification.

Getting help
You can get help by clicking Audio Help in the upper left corner of the screen. If you pause over buttons, you will hear their names and how to use them. You may want more information than Audio Help provides. If so, press F1 for Online Help.

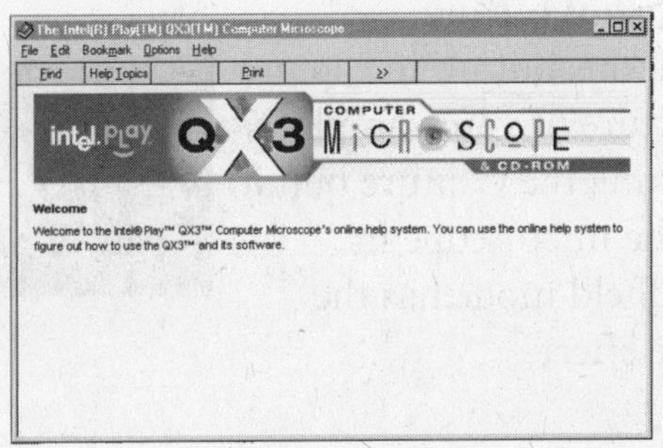

Quitting the Software

To quit, you should click the Quit button on Main. This way you can click the Cancel button to continue playing if you change your mind about quitting. (The Cancel button is on the right in the picture below.)

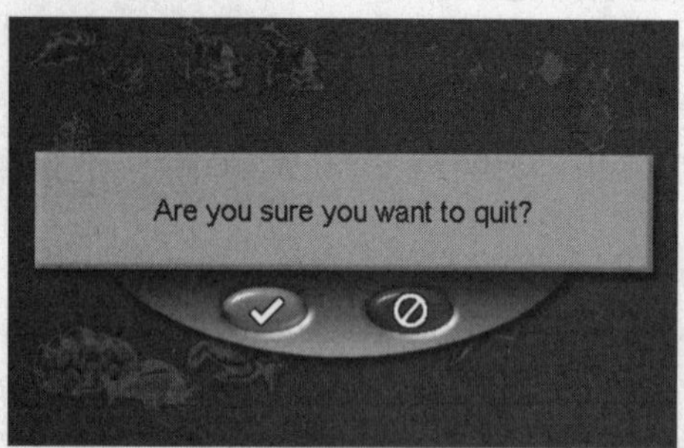
Are you sure you want to quit?

Live View

When the QX3 software starts, you're in Live View. Here you can look at things you've collected and take pictures and movies to save in your collection.

When in the Live View screen, you can:

- View samples on the sample platform or in handheld mode.
- Adjust lighting.
- Capture pictures and movies.
- Start a time-lapse movie.
- Go to Main.

Live View Buttons

Snapshot button
Click this button to capture a picture of your sample. Clicking the Capture button on the microscope in handheld mode has the same effect.

Record button
Click this button to record a movie of your sample. Holding the Capture button on the microscope in handheld mode has the same effect.

Trash Can button
Click this button to remove the last capture, shown in the preview window, from your collection.

Time Lapse button
Click this button to see the time-lapse controls.

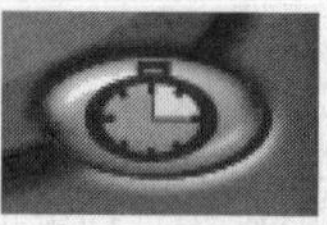

Using Handheld Mode

REMEMBER: *When using the microscope in handheld mode, don't pull on the cord that connects it to the computer. Putting too much strain on the cord can lead to trouble. Whenever you're done using the microscope in handheld mode, put it back in its cradle. Always use the microscope so that you've got a clear view of your computer monitor—so you can see what you're pointing at.*

Knowing your limits:
The main things to remember when using your microscope in handheld mode:

- Know exactly how long the cable is. If you can reach it, you can capture it with the microscope.

- Lighting automatically shifts to the top in handheld mode, but you can still adjust the brightness.

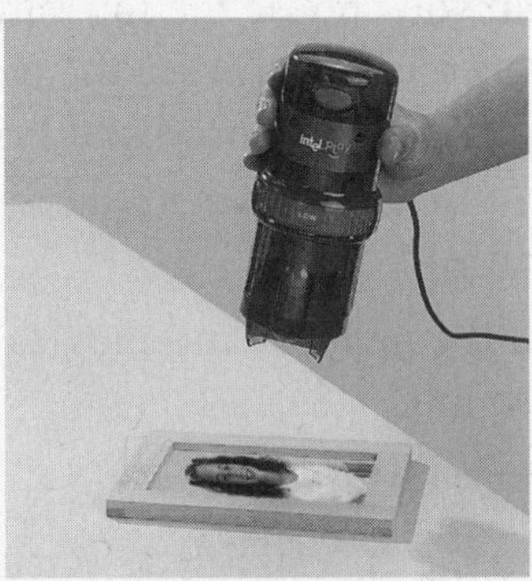

- Use low magnification unless you have plenty of light and can hold the microscope steady.
- Begin with the microscope within an inch or two of what you are looking at.
- Focus is controlled by moving the microscope closer to or farther away from the specimen. Do this slowly with small movements.

Telling your left from your right:

In a regular microscope, images are reversed. The QX3 microscope uses the software to flip the image so that when you move a slide on the sample platform to the right, the image on your monitor will also move to the right. To have this software feature work correctly in handheld mode, remember these three things:

- Hold the microscope with the magnification number facing you.
- Moving the microscope to the right is the same as moving a slide on the sample platform to the left.
- Moving the microscope toward you is the same as moving a slide on the sample platform away from you.

Making Movies

Recording indicator:

When you're capturing a movie, the bar in the Recording indicator fills up to show progress, and a counter under the Record button shows how long you have been recording. You can stop recording by clicking the Stop button. Recording will stop automatically when the status bar is full or there is no more available disk space.

Movie playback controls:
Once you've captured a movie, the Recording indicator changes into Playback controls. You preview your movie in the small window by clicking the arrow on the left side of the control. You can move through your movie one frame at a time by clicking the forward or backward arrows on the right side. To see your movie in a bigger window, go to Main and use the Playback controls.

Making a Time-Lapse Movie

Handheld mode:
With the Intel Play QX3 Computer Microscope, you can even make a time-lapse movie in handheld mode! However, the time lapse will continue only while you hold the Capture button on the microscope. When you release the button, your time lapse will end, just as if you clicked the Stop Record button on the screen. You set up a time-lapse movie in Live View. When you click the Time Lapse button, a panel opens on the bottom right side of the screen.

Time-lapse controls:
The slider controls the rate at which snapshots are taken during time-lapse experiments. As you move the slider from left to right, you can see the rate change in the display under the slider. You can set it from one picture every second to one picture every hour.

Once you've set your time lapse, you click on the Record button to start it. This puts a Minimize button in the upper right corner of the screen.

- A display under the Record button shows the total time since you started the time lapse.
- The settings control display now functions as a countdown timer to show you the length of time between snapshots.
- The display below the countdown tracks the total number of snapshots taken.

TIP: *When you're making movies of things in water, prevent condensation by leaving the lid off the containment dish. If you do a time-lapse movie that will record while you're not at the computer, make sure nobody shuts off the computer during recording. Use the Paint tools to make a warning sign. Print your warning sign and hang it on your monitor.*

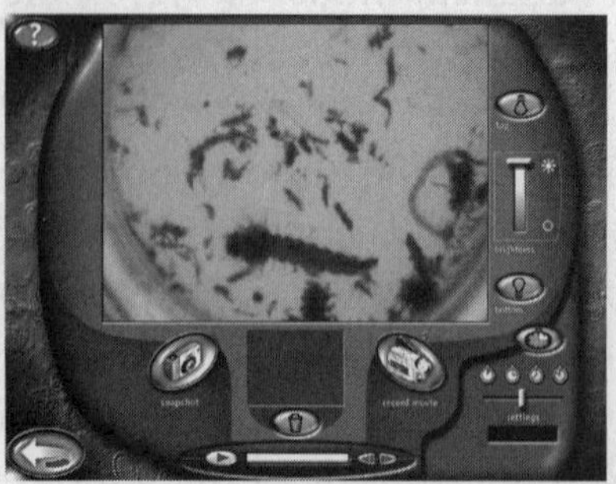

Other Software Features Available from Main

From Main you choose the software features you want to use. You will see the buttons for Paint, Special Effects, Show, and Print.

From Main you can

- View the pictures and movies in your collection.
- Go to the Paint screen.
- Go to the Special Effects screen.
- Go to the Show screen.
- Go to the Print screen.
- Return to Live View.
- Import pictures.
- Export pictures and movies.
- Delete pictures and movies from your collection.
- Quit the software.

Main buttons:

Paint button
Goes to Paint where you can modify your pictures with cool tools.

Special effects button
Takes you to a screen where you can give special effects to pictures and movies.

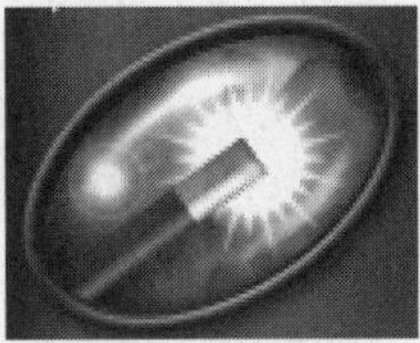

Show button
Opens one of the software's most popular features where you can assemble slide shows with music!

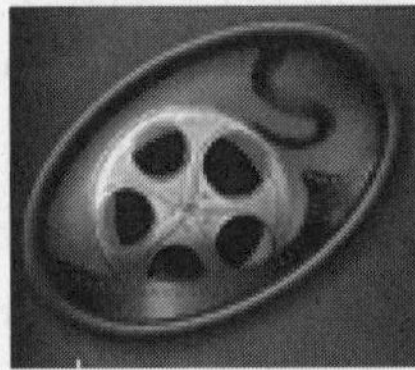

Print button
Print your pictures on a single page, on four pages to make a poster, or on stickers.

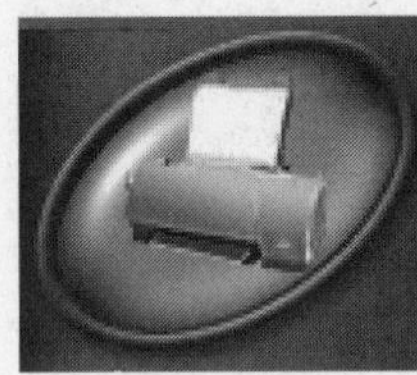

Collection button
View your collection and choose a picture or movie to look at or to use in one of the main activity screens.

Trash can button
Delete pictures and movies you no longer want. You can change your mind by clicking the Cancel button.

Quit button
When you click the Quit button, you'll get a chance to change your mind. You can't quit from within Live View. You need to go to Main to quit.

Collection window:
Look through the pictures and movies in your collection, nine at a time, by using the forward and back arrows. Movies have filmstrip borders. Once you have chosen something to work on, click OK to return to Main. You'll see your selection in the viewing area.

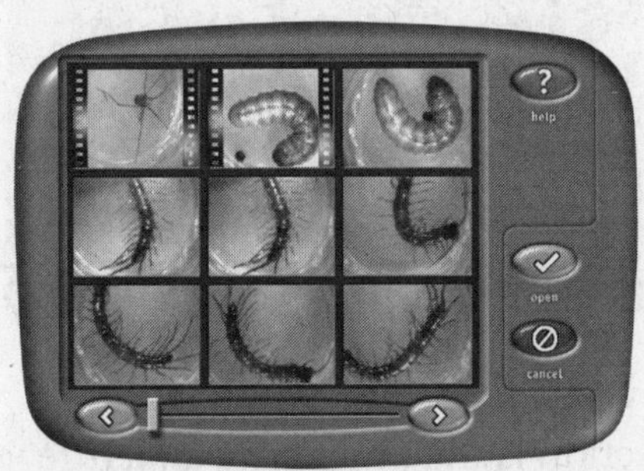

IMPORTANT: *Because the collection window opens over the top of Main, you have to click in this window for Audio Help if you need it.*

TIP: *From Main you can import still images from photo CDs and clip art collections. You can also export images and movies for use with other programs on your computer. For more information about importing and exporting, press F1 for Online Help. For more information about the controls in Main, press F1 for Online Help.*

OPERATING INSTRUCTIONS

Using Paint Tools

Paint lets you change pictures in your collection using fun tools. On Main, click the Paint button. This brings you to the Paint screen.

What is a selection?
A selection is the portion of a picture you are working with. If you don't use the Selection tool to pick an area of the picture, the entire picture is selected.

Paint tools:
Use Paint tools to change your picture. Click on a tool, and its options appear on the right side of the screen.

Scissors
Select portions of your picture to work on.

Paint brush
Control transparency, color, shape, and size of Brush Tip.

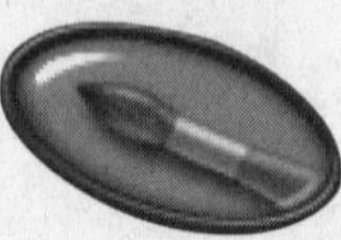

Paint bucket
Fill areas with colors and patterns. You can control whether the fill is solid or see-through.

Eyedropper
Grab a color from anywhere on your picture or the Color Palette to make it your current color.

Text
Choose the size and style before you type your text. Then click the OK button and move your text around your picture.

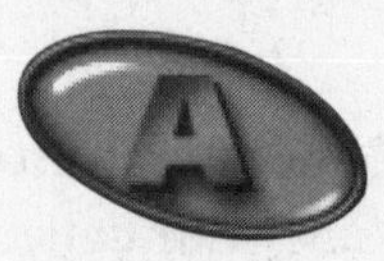

Eraser
The Eraser has four options: Erase to Original, Erase Area to Original, Erase to White, and Erase Area to White. Use Audio Help to hear more about them.

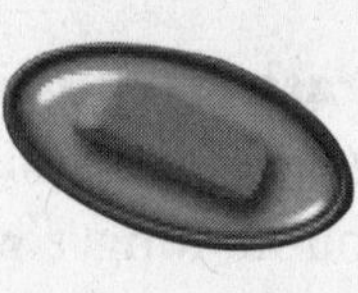

Stamp
Choose from stamp sets on the Stamp Palette. Click once on your picture to place a single random stamp from the chosen set. Click and hold while moving the mouse to spray the stamps everywhere.

Palettes, Options, and Other Controls

Scissors palette
Select parts of your picture with the rectangle or free-form Lasso. When you've made your selection, other tools work only inside that area. To work somewhere else, make a new selection. To work on the whole picture, click the De-select button.

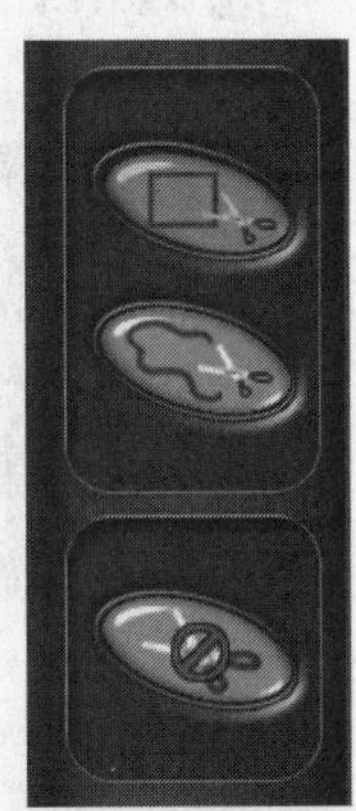

Brush tips
Click a Brush Tip shape to use it with your chosen color and pattern. Click on the up and down arrows to see more shapes and sizes. These tips can also be used with two of the erasers.

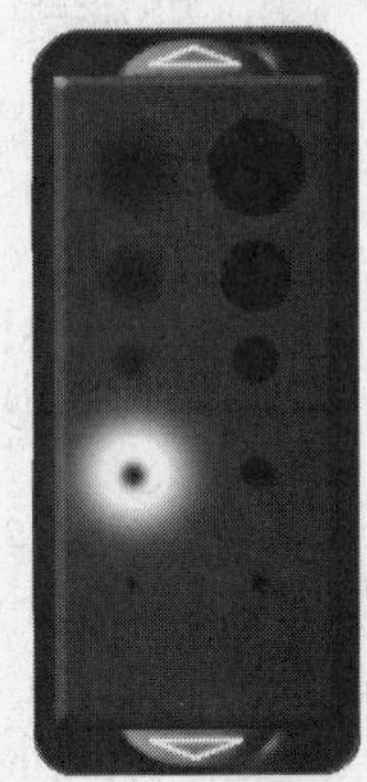

Color palette
Click anywhere on one of the color bars. Your selection is shown in the Tool Preview. You can only choose a color or a pattern, not both. You can choose colors from this palette with the Eyedropper as well.

Patterns
Click a pattern to use it. Click on the up and down arrows to see more patterns. Use the Transparency control to give your patterns unusual effects.

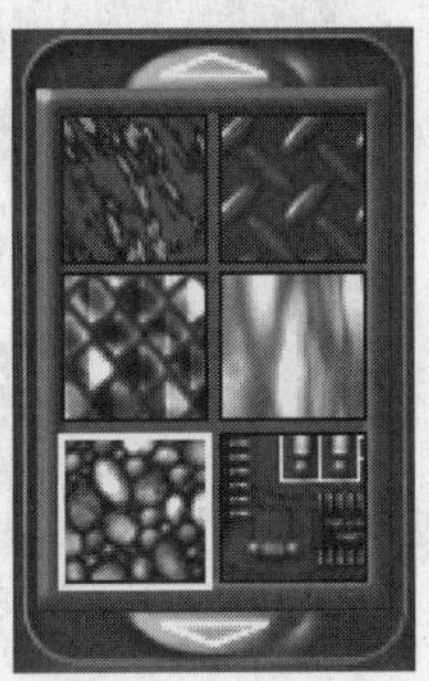

Tool preview
This box appears when you choose any tool, except Scissors or Eraser. It shows the current Color, Pattern, or Stamp set and how solid each is. The clearer the checkerboard shows, the more see-through your tool will be.

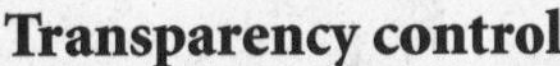

Transparency control
Use this slider to adjust how solid or see-through your tool will be. You can also use this control with Text and one of the Eraser options.

Stamp palette
Click the up and down arrows to see all the stamps you can use. Use the Transparency slider with stamps to change how see-through they are. You can even fill your words with stamps.

Picture controls
The Flip, Rotate, and Scale controls work on your current selection. Click Flip to turn your selection left to right. Move the green knob around the circle to rotate your selection. Slide the green knob on the Scale tool to make your selection bigger or smaller. If you don't have a special area selected, these tools work on your whole picture.

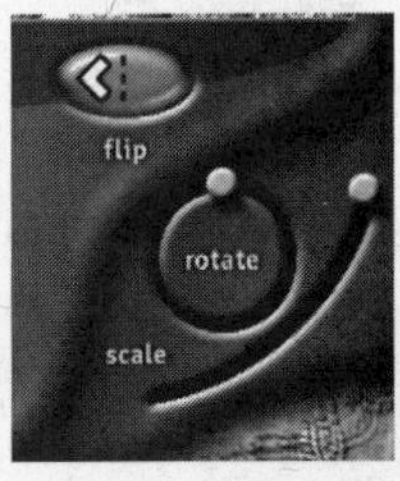

Adding Special Effects

On Main, click Special Effects. This takes you to a screen where you can give special effects to pictures and movies.

What special effects do:
Special effects change the way your picture or movie looks. There are eight effects, including Color Morph, X-Ray, Warp, Zap, Fly's Eye, Distort, Atomic Glow, Kaleidoscope, and Surprise. Surprise effect randomly applies two effects to your picture or movie. You can hear what each special effect does by using Audio Help.

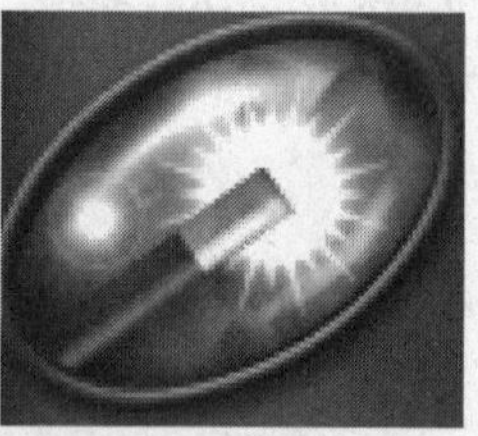

Special effects progress bar:
It takes time to apply a special effect to a movie. When the first frame is done, a Progress Bar and Cancel button appear. If you don't want to wait, you can cancel running the effect.

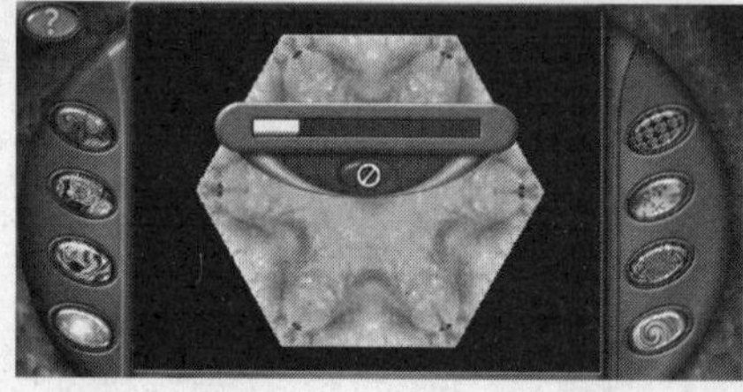

Making a Slide Show

On Main, click the Show button. This brings you to the Show screen.

Show screen:
The viewing area shows the first slide in the current show. You can have four different shows. A black window means you have opened a show with no slides in it yet. The Play Show button is also grayed if there are no slides in your current show. Each slide show can include any combination of up to 50 pictures and movies. You can even add music to your shows!

Create show:
Click here to bring up the Show Editing window. The four tabs on the right side, above the filmstrip, represent your four slide shows.

Using the show editing window:
This window acts like the Collection window. You look through your collection, nine samples at a time, by clicking on the forward and back arrows on the left side of the window. On the right side is a filmstrip with three slides from the current show. The blank green slide is always the beginning of the show, and the red slide is always the end of the show. This show is currently empty.

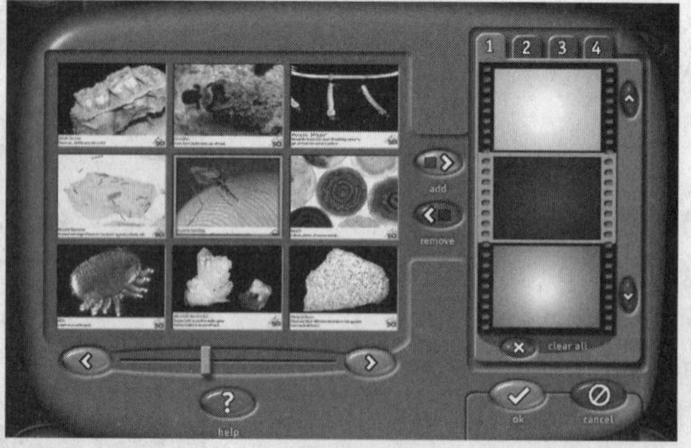

- The Add button places your selection in the middle and shifts the current slide up.
- The Remove button always cuts the middle slide and shifts the slide from above down.
- The Cancel button returns you to the Show screen without saving any changes you made to the current show.
- The OK button saves your changes and returns you to Show with the first slide in the viewing area.

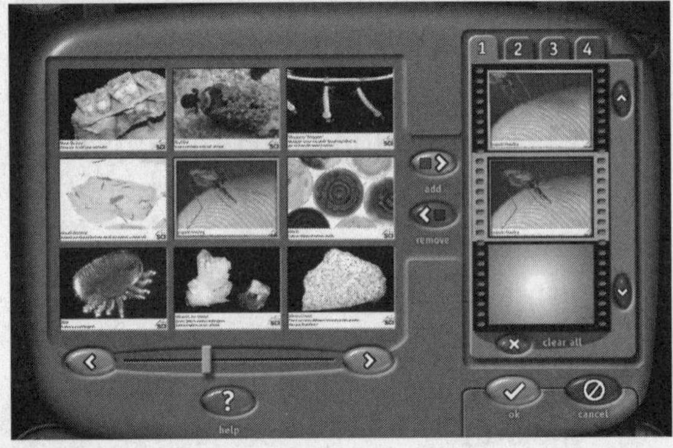

Making Your Own Slide Show

Getting ready to begin:
It's good to have a plan before putting a slide show together. Plan what you want to show, and the order you want to show it in. As you put your show together, list the pictures, movies, and text you think you need but don't have in your collection. You can either make them first or add them later.

Once you've got a plan, click the Create Show button and choose one of the tabs. If you don't have a blank tab, pick a show you want to get rid of. Click the Clear All button to empty the slides out of this show. You will see a warning, so you can change your mind. Once you have a blank show, search through your collection and add the pictures and movies you want in your new show.

If you don't like the order of your slides, you can:

- Start over with a blank show.
- Use the Add and Remove buttons to rearrange your slides.

TIP: *When you remove a slide from a show, you do not delete it from your collection. But if you delete a picture or movie from your collection, it will also disappear from any show it was in.*

Key steps in making a show:

- Search your collection by clicking the forward and back arrows below the Collection window.
- Add a slide by clicking the Add button.
- Remove a slide by moving it to the middle of the filmstrip and clicking the Remove button.
- Look through the slides in your show by using the up and down arrows.
- Click the Cancel button to leave the slide show the way it was.

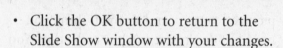

- Click the OK button to return to the Slide Show window with your changes.
- Click the Clear button to completely erase the currently selected slide show.

Playing your show:
Once you are satisfied with your show, click the OK button. You'll see the Show screen with your first slide showing. Click the Play Show button and your show will start with the first picture or movie and play over and over until you click the Pause Show button.

Adding music:
There are five kinds of music you can play while watching your show. To add or change music, click the buttons to hear short examples of the music. The last button you click before starting your show picks the music that will play with your show. To change the music during your show, just click another button. If you don't want any music, click the No Music button. It is the top button, and turns off all music.

Printing Stuff

On Main, click the Print button. This takes you to the Print screen.

Printing options:
The Print screen displays a preview of three ways to print your picture.

- Click the button under the upper left display to print a single page.
- You can print a four-page poster by clicking the button below the biggest display. You can tape the pages together and hang them on your door.

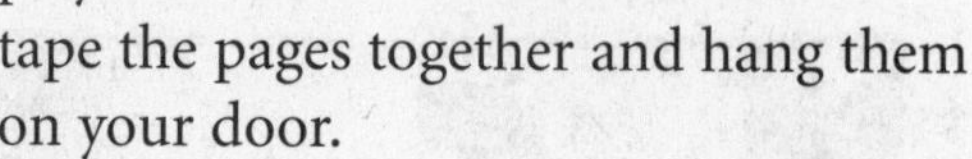

- To print a sheet of nine stickers, use special sticker paper and click the button below the display in the lower left corner of the screen.

Printing stickers:
We recommend you use Avery® Round Stickers, 3113. These are available as part of Avery Personal Creations White Removable Stickers Variety Pack, 3274.

Important Changes

Check the Read Me file for important changes and information developed since this guide was printed.

System Information Utility

The QX3 microscope includes a system information utility to assist in solving any problems you may be having with your microscope. If you need to contact technical support, you may be asked to run this program from the Windows Start Menu to produce a report.

Universal Serial Bus (USB) Problems

If your microscope shows up in the device manager as disabled or nonfunctioning, you can check the Intel Play support web site (http://www.intelplay.com) for up-to-date information on USB problems and solutions. You may be asked to run the system information utility to isolate and solve the problem.

Sluggish Performance

If you have trouble focusing, or other operations seem excessively slow, set your screen color depth to 24- or 16-bit color (if available). This decreases the processing load. You should also Alt-Tab to other open applications and close them.

Hard Disk Space

The software indicates when hard drive space is low and prevents new samples from being created until more space is available. The minimum amount of free disk space needed is 20 Megabytes.

NOTE: *A 90-second real-time movie will use approximately 4.8 MB of disk space. Each snapshot will use between 270 to 650 KB of disk space.*

Visual Orientation Confusion

In handheld mode, moving the QX3 microscope toward you has the same effect as pushing a slide on the sample platform away from you. Likewise, moving to the right in handheld mode is the same as moving a slide on the sample platform to the left. Press F1 for Online Help for additional information.

Special Effects

The time it takes to apply a special effect depends on the complexity of the sample being altered, the effect chosen, and your computer model. The faster the computer, the more quickly an effect will render. Movies are processed one frame at a time. Applying a complex effect to a long movie can take considerable time. For this reason, you are given the opportunity to cancel effects applied to movies. Canceling an effect leaves your original sample untouched.

Sound

We recommend using speakers that connect directly to the ports on your sound card. Although USB speakers work with the QX3 software, under heavy CPU load we have found quality problems, resulting in choppy playback.

Import/export problems

Import supports the following formats:

- BMP (1-bit, 2-bit, 4-bit, 8-bit, 24-bit, and 32-bit color depths).
- JPEG (color and gray scale).
- Photo CD.

Export supports the following formats:

- BMP (24-bit), JPEG (color).
- AVI.

Error Messages

You may encounter error messages using the QX3 software. These errors will appear either in the Live View screen or in a standard dialog box on problems and solutions.

Error messages appearing in a standard dialog box contain a number to identify the specific cause to technical support. These messages also include a suggested resolution. The following table lists the most common of these messages and additional suggested solutions.

Message	Solution
Your microscope is not plugged in.	Connect the microscope; see Setup Guide.
Your computer can't find all the necessary software components.	Reinstall the QX3 software. Or go to Add/Remove Programs in your computer's control panel, select the QX3 microscope from the menu of programs, and click Add/Remove. Select the "repair" option and click "next."
There is not enough room on your computer to get started.	Delete items from the sample collection, run the Windows maintenance utilities, and/or delete other unused files and applications. If your computer matches the minimum system requirements, contact Technical Support.
Your computer can't run this program.	Click OK to exit the software. Restart the QX3 software. If the error repeats, reboot your computer.
Your computer stopped paying attention.	Alt-tab to other open applications and Exit them.
You are out of memory.	Please exit other applications to free up more memory.

Contact Neo/SCI for Technical Support at: 1-800-526-6689 or **www.neosci.com**

SCIENCE SAFETY RULES

To prepare yourself to work safely in the laboratory, read over the following safety rules. Then read them a second time. Make sure you understand and follow each rule. Ask your teacher to explain any rules you do not understand.

Dress Code

1. To protect yourself from injuring your eyes, wear safety goggles whenever you work with chemicals, flames, glassware, or any substance that might get into your eyes. If you wear contact lenses, notify your teacher.
2. Wear an apron or coat whenever you work with corrosive chemicals or substances that can stain.
3. Tie back long hair to keep it away from any chemicals, flames, or equipment.
4. Remove or tie back any article of clothing or jewelry that can hang down and touch chemicals, flames, or equipment. Roll up or secure long sleeves.
5. Never wear open shoes or sandals.

General Precautions

6. Read all directions for an experiment several times before beginning the activity. Carefully follow all written and oral instructions. If you are in doubt about any part of the experiment, ask your teacher for assistance.
7. Never perform activities that are not assigned or authorized by your teacher. Obtain permission before "experimenting" on your own. Never handle any equipment unless you have specific permission.
8. Never perform lab activities without direct supervision.
9. Never eat or drink in the laboratory.
10. Keep work areas clean and tidy at all times. Bring only notebooks and lab manuals or written lab procedures to the work area. All other items, such as purses and backpacks, should be left in a designated area.
11. Do not engage in horseplay.

First Aid

12. Always report all accidents or injuries to your teacher, no matter how minor. Notify your teacher immediately about any fires.
13. Learn what to do in case of specific accidents, such as getting acid in your eyes or on your skin. (Rinse acids from your body with plenty of water.)
14. Be aware of the location of the first-aid kit, but do not use it unless instructed by your teacher. In case of injury, your teacher should administer first aid. Your teacher may also send you to the school nurse or call a physician.
15. Know the location of the emergency equipment such as fire extinguisher and fire blanket.
16. Know the location of the nearest telephone and whom to contact in an emergency.

Heating and Fire Safety

17. Never use a heat source, such as a candle, burner, or hot plate, without wearing safety goggles.
18. Never heat anything unless instructed to do so. A chemical that is harmless when cool may be dangerous when heated.
19. Keep all combustible materials away from flames. Never use a flame or spark near a combustible chemical.
20. Never reach across a flame.

SCIENCE SAFETY RULES

21. Before using a laboratory burner, make sure you know proper procedures for lighting and adjusting the burner, as demonstrated by your teacher. Do not touch the burner. It may be hot. Never leave a lighted burner unattended. Turn off the burner when not in use.
22. Chemicals can splash or boil out of a heated test tube. When heating a substance in a test tube, make sure that the mouth of the tube is not pointed at you or anyone else.
23. Never heat a liquid in a closed container. The expanding gases produced may shatter the container.
24. Before picking up a container that has been heated, first hold the back of your hand near it. If you can feel heat on the back of your hand, the container is too hot to handle. Use an oven mitt to pick up a container that has been heated.

Using Chemicals Safely

25. Never mix chemicals "for the fun of it." You might produce a dangerous, possibly explosive substance.
26. Never put your face near the mouth of a container that holds chemicals. Many chemicals are poisonous. Never touch, taste, or smell a chemical unless you are instructed by your teacher to do so.
27. Use only those chemicals needed in the activity. Read and double-check labels on supply bottles before removing any chemicals. Take only as much as you need. Keep all containers closed when chemicals are not being used.
28. Dispose of all chemicals as instructed by your teacher. To avoid contamination, never return chemicals to their original containers. Never pour untreated chemicals or other substances into the sink or trash containers.
29. Be extra careful when working with acids or bases. Pour all chemicals over the sink or a container, not over your work surface.
30. If you are instructed to test for odors, use a wafting motion to direct the odors to your nose. Do not inhale the fumes directly from the container.
31. When mixing an acid and water, always pour the water into the container first then add the acid to the water. Never pour water into an acid.
32. Take extreme care not to spill any material in the laboratory. Wash chemical spills and splashes immediately with plenty of water. Immediately begin rinsing with water any acids that get on your skin or clothing, and notify your teacher of any acid spill at the same time.

Using Glassware Safely

33. Never force glass tubing or a thermometer into a rubber stopper or rubber tubing. Have your teacher insert the glass tubing or thermometer if required for an activity.
34. If you are using a laboratory burner, use a wire screen to protect glassware from any flame. Never heat glassware that is not thoroughly dry on the outside.
35. Keep in mind that hot glassware looks cool. Never pick up glassware without first checking to see if it is hot. Use an oven mitt. See rule 24.
36. Never use broken or chipped glassware. If glassware breaks, notify your teacher and dispose of the glassware in the proper broken-glassware container.
37. Never eat or drink from glassware.
38. Thoroughly clean glassware before putting it away.

SCIENCE SAFETY RULES

Using Sharp Instruments

39. Handle scalpels or other sharp instruments with extreme care. Never cut material toward you; cut away from you.

40. Immediately notify your teacher if you cut your skin when working in the laboratory.

Animal and Plant Safety

41. Never perform experiments that cause pain, discomfort, or harm to animals. This rule applies at home as well as in the classroom.

42. Animals should be handled only if absolutely necessary. Your teacher will instruct you as to how to handle each animal species brought into the classroom.

43. If you know that you are allergic to certain plants, molds, or animals, tell your teacher before doing an activity in which these are used.

44. During field work, protect your skin by wearing long pants, long sleeves, socks, and closed shoes. Know how to recognize the poisonous plants and fungi in your area, as well as plants with thorns, and avoid contact with them. Never eat any part of a plant or fungus.

45. Wash your hands thoroughly after handling animals or a cage containing animals. Wash your hands when you are finished with any activity involving animal parts, plants, or soil.

End-of-Experiment Rules

46. After an experiment has been completed, turn off all burners or hot plates. If you used a gas burner, check that the gas-line valve to the burner is off. Unplug hot plates.

47. Turn off and unplug any other electrical equipment that you used.

48. Clean up your work area and return all equipment to its proper place.

49. Dispose of waste materials as instructed by your teacher.

50. Wash your hands after every experiment.

Intel® Play™ QX3™ Computer Microscope
Prentice Hall Science Explorer Edition

PRENTICE HALL SCIENCE EXPLORER

SAFETY SYMBOLS

These symbols alert you to possible dangers in the laboratory and remind you to work carefully.

Safety Goggles Always wear safety goggles to protect your eyes in any activity involving chemicals, flames or heating, or the possibility of broken glassware.

Lab Apron Wear a laboratory apron to protect your skin and clothing from damage.

Breakage You are working with materials that may be breakable, such as glass containers, glass tubing, thermometers, or funnels. Handle breakable materials with care. Do not touch broken glassware.

Heat-Resistant Gloves Use an oven mitt or other hand protection when handling hot materials. Hot plates, hot glassware, or hot water can cause burns. Do not touch hot objects with your bare hands.

Heating Use a clamp or tongs to pick up hot glassware. Do not touch hot objects with your bare hands.

Sharp Object Pointed-tip scissors, scalpels, knives, needles, pins, or tacks are sharp. They can cut or puncture your skin. Always direct a sharp edge or point away from yourself and others. Use sharp instruments only as instructed.

Electric Shock Avoid the possibility of electric shock. Never use electrical equipment around water, or when the equipment is wet or your hands are wet. Be sure cords are untangled and cannot trip anyone. Disconnect the equipment when it is not in use.

Corrosive Chemical You are working with an acid or another corrosive chemical. Avoid getting it on your skin or clothing, or in your eyes. Do not inhale the vapors. Wash your hands when you are finished with the activity.

Poison Do not let any poisonous chemical come in contact with your skin, and do not inhale its vapors. Wash your hands when you are finished with the activity.

Physical Safety When an experiment involves physical activity, take precautions to avoid injuring yourself or others. Follow instructions from the teacher. Alert the teacher if there is any reason you should not participate in the activity.

Animal Safety Treat live animals with care to avoid harming the animals or yourself. Working with animal parts or preserved animals also requires caution. Wash your hands when you are finished with the activity.

Plant Safety Handle plants in the laboratory or during field work only as directed by the teacher. If you are allergic to certain plants, tell the teacher before doing an activity in which those plants are used. Avoid touching harmful plants such as poison ivy, poison oak, or poison sumac, or plants with thorns. Wash your hands when you are finished with the activity.

Flames You may be working with flames from a lab burner, candle, or matches. Tie back loose hair and clothing. Follow instructions from the teacher about lighting and extinguishing flames.

No Flames Flammable materials may be present. Make sure there are no flames, sparks, or other exposed heat sources present.

Fumes When poisonous or unpleasant vapors may be involved, work in a ventilated area. Avoid inhaling vapors directly. Only test an odor when directed to do so by the teacher, and use a wafting motion to direct the vapor toward your nose.

Disposal Chemicals and other laboratory materials used in the activity must be disposed of safely. Follow the instructions from the teacher.

Hand Washing Wash your hands thoroughly when finished with the activity. Use antibacterial soap and warm water. Lather both sides of your hands and between your fingers. Rinse well.

General Safety Awareness You may see this symbol when none of the symbols described earlier appears. In this case, follow the specific instructions provided. You may also see this symbol when you are asked to develop your own procedure in a lab. Have the teacher approve your plan before you go further.

LAB SAFETY CONTRACT

I, ____, have read the Science Safety Rules
(please print full name)

and Safety Symbols sections in this manual, understand their contents completely, and agree to demonstrate compliance with all safety rules and guidelines that have been established in each of the following categories:

(please check)

- ❑ Dress Code
- ❑ General Precautions
- ❑ First Aid
- ❑ Heating and Fire Safety
- ❑ Using Chemicals Safely
- ❑ Using Glassware Safely
- ❑ Using Sharp Instruments
- ❑ Animal and Plant Safety
- ❑ End-of-Experiment Rules

____
(signature)

Date ________________________

Teacher Notes

Name ______________________ Date __________ Class ______________

L1 **TRY THIS**

React!

◆ Background

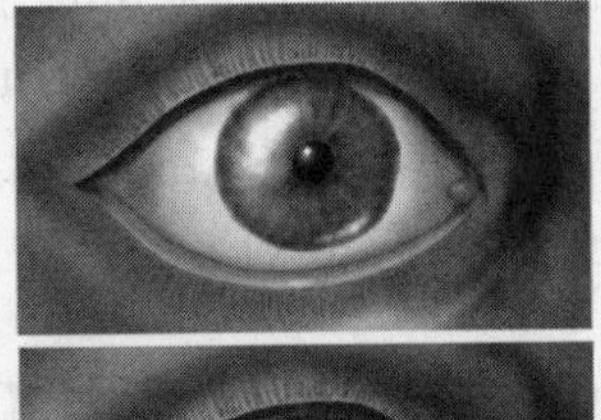
Eye response to light

Eye response to darkness

All organisms react to changes in their environment. A change in an organism's surroundings that causes the organism to react is called a stimulus (plural stimuli). External stimuli come from outside the organism. External stimuli include things, such as light, sound, and the temperature of the environment.

◆ Skills Objective

You will be able to:

- classify changes in an object in response to an external stimulus.

◆ Using the QX3 Microscope you Will...

Make a movie that demonstrates the human eye's response to light.
Capture macro images of external eye anatomy.

◆ Materials

QX3 microscope
clear plastic ruler

◆ Safety Tips   *Review the safety guidelines in the front of your lab book.*

Do not look directly at the light on the QX3 microscope.

◆ Procedure

1. Work in pairs for this exercise. One partner will be the "subject." The other partner will be the "data collector" and will capture the images on the QX3 microscope. You can change roles at the end of the exercise, so that each person has an image of his or her own eye.
2. The subject should hold the QX3 microscope so that the light just touches one of his or her eyebrows. Look straight ahead and slightly downward.
3. The subject may move the QX3 microscope around slowly until the data collector indicates that the subject's eye is centered on the computer screen.
4. The subject should then remain motionless while the data collector captures a snapshot of the subject's eye.
5. The recorder should now begin to record a real-time movie while the subject blinks several times. Stop recording.

LIFE SCIENCE

Name ______________________ Date __________ Class ______________

6. Now the subject should hold his or her eyes shut tight for three seconds and then rapidly open them. The recorder should take a snapshot of the subject's eyes immediately after opening. The subject should now hold the eyes wide open for three seconds. The recorder should take a second snapshot.
7. Measure the diameter of the subject's pupil in each snapshot, and record the data in the Data Collection and Observations section.

◆ Data Collection and Observations

Condition	Pupil Diameter (mm)
Immediately after opening eye	
After holding eye open for 3 seconds	

LIFE SCIENCE

◆ Analyze and Conclude

1. What happened to the diameter of the pupil when it was exposed to light?

____

____

2. What was the stimulus in this exercise? Was the stimulus internal or external?

____

____

3. What was the response in this exercise?

____

____

◆ Going Further

Take a snapshot of the external anatomical features of the eye and label the snapshot with the appropriate structure names and their functions. Construct a poster relating the eye structures with their functions.

Name ______________________ Date ____________ Class ______________

L2 **SKILLS LAB**

Please Pass the Bread!

◆ Background

Organisms that cannot make their own food are called heterotrophs. Hetero- means "other." Animals, mushrooms, and bread mold are examples of heterotrophs. Heterotrophs either eat autotrophs and obtain energy in the autotroph's stored food, or they consume other heterotrophs that eat autotrophs. A heterotroph's energy source is also the sun—but in an indirect way.

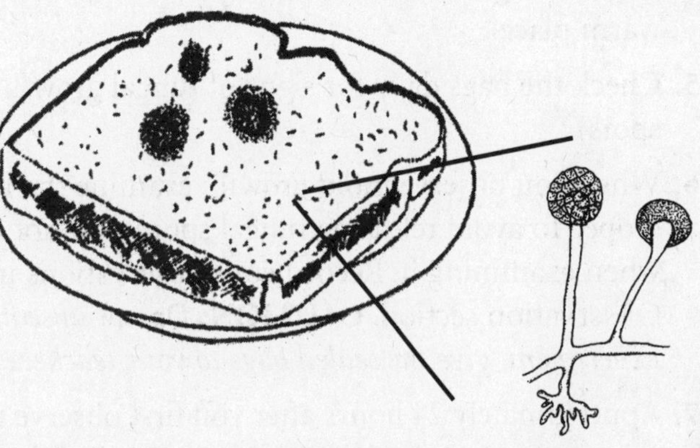

Common Bread Mold

◆ Skills Objectives

You will be able to:

- control variables to determine the effects of different factors;
- draw conclusions about how various factors affect the growth of bread mold.

◆ Using the QX3 Microscope you Will...

Capture images of bread mold.
Make time-lapse movies of the growth of bread mold.

◆ Materials

QX3 microscope
bread without preservatives
tap water
plastic dropper
sealable plastic bags
packing tape

◆ Safety Tips   *Review the safety guidelines in the front of your lab book.*

To prevent spore release, do not open the plastic bags.

◆ Procedure

1. Predict which factors might affect the growth of bread mold. Record your ideas in your lab notebook.
2. To test the effect of moisture on the growth of bread mold, place two slices of bread of the same size and thickness on separate, clean, paper towels.

LIFE SCIENCE

Name ______________________ Date __________ Class __________

PLEASE PASS THE BREAD *(continued)*

3. Add drops of tap water to one bread slice until the whole slice is moist. Keep the other slice dry. Expose both slices to the air for 1 hour.
4. Put each slice into its own bag. Press the outside of each bag to remove the air. Seal the bags. Then use packing tape to seal the bags again. Store the bags in a warm place.
5. Check the bags daily for signs of fungal growth (fuzzy, whitish areas with black spots).
6. When you observe mold growth, examine the mold using the QX3 microscope. To avoid releasing fungal spores, do not remove the bread from the bag when examining it. Record your observations in the Data Collection and Observation section. **CAUTION:** *Do not unseal the bags. At the end of the experiment, give the sealed bags to your teacher.*
7. Approximately 24 hours after you first observe mold growth, set up the QX3 microscope to record a time-lapse movie of the fungus. Set the time-lapse recording intervals for every 15 minutes. Leave the QX3 microscope undisturbed overnight. The mold spores will change in color as pigment is produced.

LIFE SCIENCE

◆ Data Collection and Observations

	Moistened Bread Slice		Unmoistened Bread Slice	
	Mold Present?	**Area with Mold**	**Mold Present?**	**Area with Mold**
Day 1				
Day 2				
Day 3				
Day 4				
Day 5				
Day 6				
Day 7				

◆ Analyze and Conclude

1. What conclusions can you draw from your experiment?

____

____

Name ______________________ Date __________ Class ______________

PLEASE PASS THE BREAD *(continued)*

2. What was the variable in this experiment?

3. What basic needs of living things were demonstrated in this lab? Explain.

4. What is meant by "controlling the variables"? Why is it necessary to control variables in an experiment?

◆ Going Further

Try using different varieties of bread (made with and without preservatives, or with different types of flour), and place them under different conditions. Try to determine if flour type, humidity, or temperature influence mold growth. Make a poster that shows the results of this experiment.

Name ______________________ Date ____________ Class ______________

L3 **DISCOVER**

Is Seeing Believing?

◆ Background

Microscopes use lenses to make small objects look larger. However, simply enlarging small objects is not useful unless you can see the details clearly. For a microscope to be useful to a scientist, it must combine two important properties—magnification and resolution. Magnification is the ability to make things look larger than they are. The ability to clearly distinguish the individual parts of an object is called resolution. Resolution is another term for the sharpness of an image.

◆ Skills Objective

You will be able to:

- observe the effect resolution in enlargements.

LIFE SCIENCE

◆ Using the QX3 Microscope you Will...

Capture images of newspaper photographs.

◆ Materials

QX3 microscope
hand lens
newsprint
newspaper photographs

◆ Safety Tip

Review the safety guidelines in the front of your lab book.

◆ Procedure

1. Cut a black and white photograph out of a page in a newspaper. With your eyes alone, closely examine the photo. Record your observations in the Data Collection and Observations section.
2. Examine the same photo with a hand lens. Record your observations in the Data Collection and Observations section.
3. Place the photo on the stage of the QX3 microscope. Use top lighting, and set the magnification to 60X. Focus the lens and examine the photo. Take a snapshot of the magnified photo. Record your observations in the Data Collection and Observations section.

Name ____________________ Date __________ Class ____________

IS SEEING BELIEVING? *(continued)*

◆ Data Collection and Observations

Observations with eyes only	
Observations with hand lens	
Observations with QX3 microscope	

◆ Analyze and Conclude

1. What did you see in the photo with the hand lens and the QX3 microscope that you could not see with your eyes alone?

____

____

2. To the eye, paper appears to have a smooth texture. What did you observe about the microscopic texture of newspaper?

____

____

◆ Going Further

Make predictions about the microscopic appearances of wax paper, glossy magazine print, and photographic paper. Check your predictions using the QX3 microscope.

LIFE SCIENCE

Name ______________________ Date __________ Class ______________

L 4 SHARPEN YOUR SKILLS

Observing

◆ Background

One of the first people to observe cells was the English scientist and inventor, Robert Hooke. In 1663, Hooke observed the structure of a thin slice of cork using a compound microscope he had built himself. Cork, the bark of the cork oak tree, is made up of cells that are no longer alive. To Hooke, the cork looked like tiny rectangular rooms, which he called cells.

◆ Skills Objectives

You will be able to:

- observe and draw cells and organisms.

LIFE SCIENCE

◆ Using the QX3 Microscope you Will...

Capture images of thin slices of cork and various living cells.

◆ Materials

QX3 microscope
prepared slide of cork cells
lettuce
water
pond water
plastic dropper
slide
cover slip

◆ Safety Tips   *Review the safety guidelines in the front of your lab book.*

◆ Procedure

1. Place a prepared slide of a thin slice of cork on the stage of the QX3 microscope.
2. Observe the slide under 60X magnification. Count the number of cells that fit end to end in the field of view. Draw what you see through the microscope in the Data Collection and Observations section. Take a snapshot.
3. Put a small, very thick piece of lettuce on a slide. Repeat Step 2.
4. Place a few drops of pond water on another slide and cover it with a coverslip. Repeat Step 2.
5. Wash your hands after handling pond water.

Name ______________________ Date __________ Class ______________

OBSERVING *(continued)*

◆ Data Collection and Observations

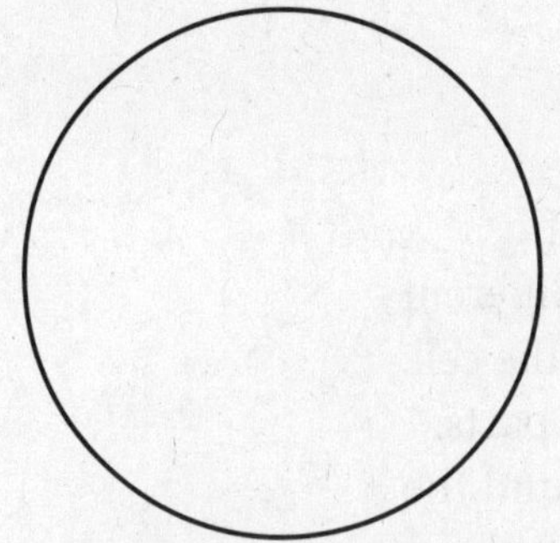
Cork cell drawing

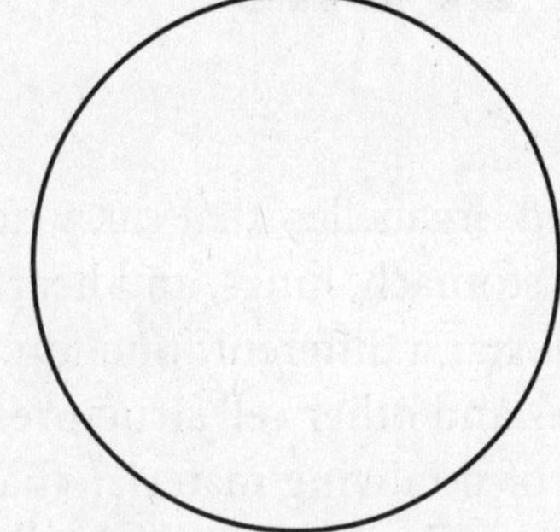
Lettuce cell drawing

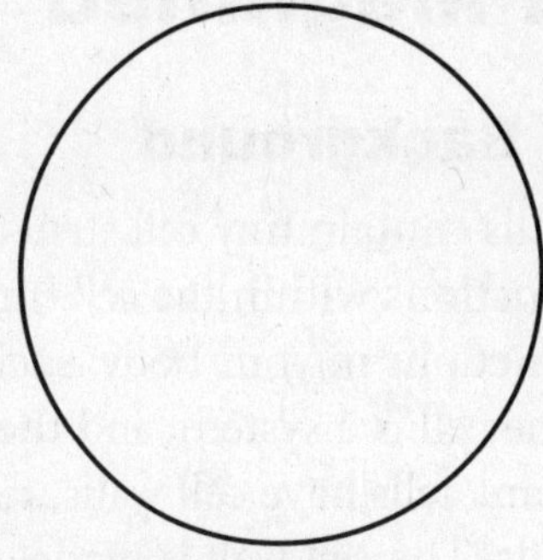
Pond water drawing

	Cork	Lettuce
# Cells that fit across field of view		

LIFE SCIENCE

◆ Analyze and Conclude

1. How does your drawing of cork cells compare to Hooke's drawing in your textbook?

____

____

2. Based upon your observations of pond water, why did Leeuwenhoek call the organisms he saw "little animals"?

____

____

◆ Going Further

Make a poster of cells using the snapshots you took with the QX3 microscope. Label snapshots with the source of the cells.

Name ______________________ Date __________ Class __________

L5 SKILLS LAB

A Magnified View of Life

◆ Background

Cells contain tiny cell structures, called organelles, that carry out specific functions within the cell. Just as your stomach, lungs, and heart have different functions in your body, each organelle has a different function within the cell. The cell is a system, and the organelles and other cell structures are its parts. Plant cells have cell walls, rigid layers of nonliving material, that surround the cells. The cell wall is made of a tough, yet flexible, material called cellulose. In contrast, the cells of animals and some other organisms lack cell walls.

◆ Skills Objectives

LIFE SCIENCE

You will be able to:

- observe and draw cells under the microscope;
- compare and contrast plant and animal cells.

◆ Using the QX3 Microscope you Will...

Capture images of plant and animal cells.
Create a movie showing organelle movement in *Elodea* cells.

◆ Materials

QX3 microscope
plastic dropper
water
microscope slide
colored pencils
prepared animal cell slide
Elodea leaf
forceps
coverslip

◆ Safety Tips     

Review the safety guidelines in the front of your lab book.

Name ______________________ Date __________ Class ______________

A MAGNIFIED VIEW OF LIFE *(continued)*

◆ Procedure

Part 1: Observing Plant Cells

1. Use a plastic dropper to place a drop of water in the center of the slide.
2. With forceps, remove a leaf from an *Elodea* plant. Place the leaf in the drop of water on the slide. Make sure that the leaf is flat. If it is folded, straighten it out with the forceps.
3. Holding a coverslip by its edges, slowly lower it onto the drop of water and *Elodea* leaf. If any air bubbles form, tap the slide gently to get rid of them.
4. Examine the *Elodea* leaf with the QX3 microscope at 10X magnification. Then, switch to 60X magnification and examine the leaf again. Finally, switch to 200X magnification.
5. Observe the cells of the *Elodea* leaf. In the Data Collection and Observations section, draw and label what you see, including the colors of the cell parts. Take a snapshot that you can label for a poster.
6. Continue to observe the *Elodea* cells. You may notice some of the cell contents moving about within the cell. If you see the cytoplasm and organelles moving within the cells, make a short movie of this movement.
7. Discard the *Elodea* leaf as directed by your teacher. Carefully clean and dry your slide and coverslip. Wash your hands thoroughly.

Part 2: Observing Animal Cells

8. Obtain a prepared slide of animal cells. The cells on the slide have been stained with an artificial color.
9. Observe the animal cells with the QX3 microscope at 10X, 60X, and 200X magnification. In the Data Collection and Observations section, draw and label the cell parts that you see. Take a snapshot of the cells that you can label for a poster.

◆ Data Collection and Observations

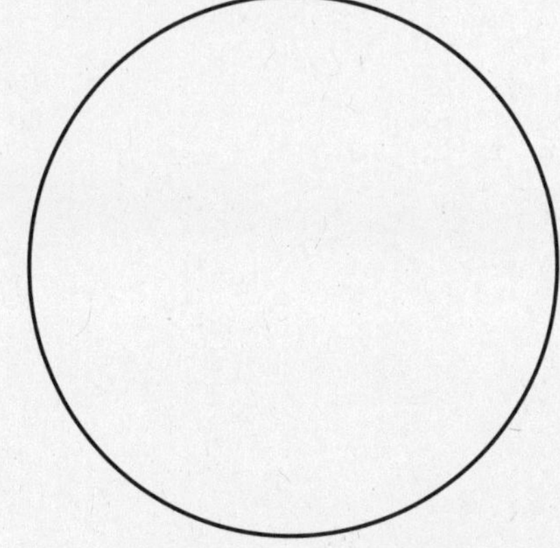

Plant Cells (200X)

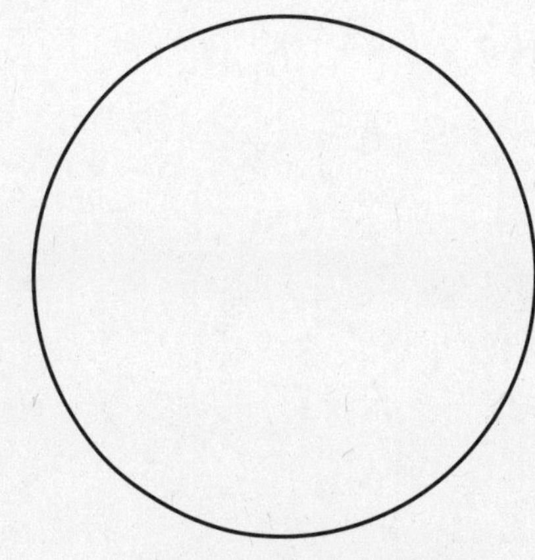

Animal Cells (200X)

LIFE SCIENCE

Name ______________________ Date __________ Class ______________

A MAGNIFIED VIEW OF LIFE *(continued)*

◆ Analyze and Conclude

1. How are plant and animal cells alike?

2. How are plant and animal cells different?

3. What natural color appeared in the plant cells? What structures give the plant cells this color?

4. Why is it important to record your observations while you are examining a specimen?

◆ Going Further

Place a microscope slide flat on the counter on a piece of paper towel. Use a plastic dropper to place a drop of water on the center of the slide. Position your hand or forearm over the drop of water on the slide, and scrape the skin gently with a fingernail so that some skin cells fall into the drop of water. Add a drop of methylene blue stain or iodine to the drop of water with skin cells on the slide. Add a coverslip. Observe your slide at 10X to locate the skin cells. Then switch to higher magnification to see more detail. Take a snapshot.

Name ______________________ Date __________ Class __________

L6 SKILLS LAB

Multiplying by Dividing

◆ Background

Each cell contains many different structures, including a cell membrane, a nucleus, mitochondria, and ribosomes. To divide into two equal parts, the cell would need to either duplicate the structures or divide them equally between the two new cells. Both cells would then contain everything they need in order to function. The regular sequence of growth and division that cells undergo is known as the cell cycle. The cell cycle is divided into three main stages called interphase, mitosis, and cytokinesis.

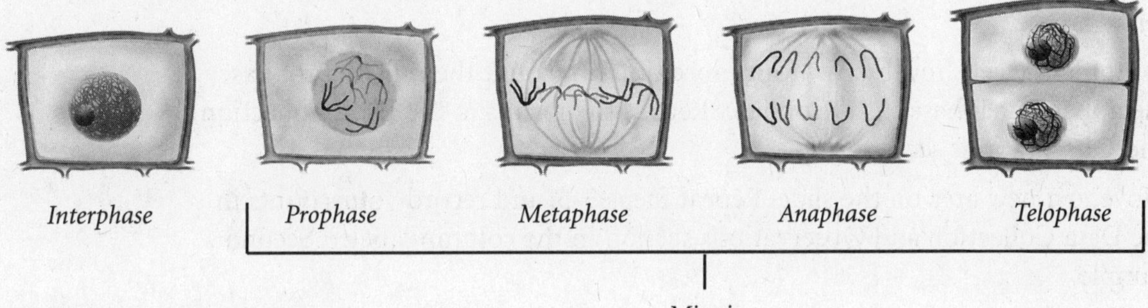

◆ Skills Objectives

You will be able to:

- observe cells in different stages of the cell cycle;
- calculate the amount of time cells spend in each stage of the cell cycle;
- interpret data to compare how long cells spend in mitosis with the total time of the cell cycle.

◆ Using the QX3 Microscope you Will...

Capture images of the stages of mitosis in plant cells.

◆ Materials

QX3 microscope
colored pencils
calculator
prepared slide of onion root tip cells undergoing cell division

◆ Safety Tips  *Review the safety guidelines in the front of your lab book.*

LIFE SCIENCE

Name ______________________ Date ____________ Class ____________

MULTIPLYING BY DIVIDING *(continued)*

◆ Procedure

1. Place the slide on the stage of the QX3 microscope. Use 10X magnification to locate a cell in interphase. Switch to 200X magnification, and make a labeled drawing of the cell in the Data Collection and Observations section. Take a snapshot.
2. Repeat Step 1 to find cells in prophase, metaphase, anaphase, and telophase. Take snapshots of each phase.
3. Return to 10X magnification. Find an area with many cells dividing. Switch to the magnification that lets you see about 50 cells (at either 60X or 200X).
4. Examine the cells row by row, and count the cells that are in interphase. Record that number in the Data Collection and Observations section under First Sample.
5. Examine the cells row by row four more times to count the cells in prophase, metaphase, anaphase, and telophase. Record the results in the Data Collection and Observations section.
6. Move to a new area on the slide. Repeat Steps 3-5, and record your counts in the Data Collection and Observations section in the column labeled Second Sample.
7. In the Data Collection and Observations section, fill in the column labeled Total Number by adding the numbers across each row.
8. Add the totals for the five stages to find the total number of cells counted.

LIFE SCIENCE

◆ Data Collection and Observations

DATA TABLE

Stages of Cell Cycle	First Sample	Second Sample	Total Number
Interphase			
Mitosis: Prophase			
Metaphase			
Anaphase			
Telophase			
Total Number of Cells Counted			

Name ______________________ Date __________ Class ______________

MULTIPLYING BY DIVIDING *(continued)*

◆ Analyze and Conclude

1. Which stage of the cell cycle did you observe most often?

____

2. The cell cycle for onion root tips takes about 720 minutes (12 hours). Use your data and the formula below to find the number of minutes each stage takes. Do your calculations with a pencil and paper, a calculator, or a computer.

$$\text{Time for each stage} = \frac{\text{Number of cells at each stage}}{\text{Total number of cells counted}} \times 720 \text{ min}$$

3. Compare the amount of time spent in mitosis with the total time for the whole cell cycle.

____

____

◆ Going Further

Make a poster of the labeled snapshots you took of the plant cells. Be sure to place all of the mitotic stages in their proper order with respect to each other and the other stages in the cell cycle.

LIFE SCIENCE

Name ______________________ Date __________ Class ______________

L7 DISCOVER

What Do Fingerprints Reveal?

◆ Background

In courtrooms across the country, a genetic technique called DNA fingerprinting is being used to help solve crimes. In this activity, you will learn that fingerprints can help to identify people. No two people have the same fingerprints. Detectives routinely use fingerprints found at a crime scene to help identify the person who committed the crime. In a similar way, DNA from samples of hair, skin, and blood can also be used to identify a person. No two people, except for identical twins, have the same DNA.

Plain Whorl

Radial Loop

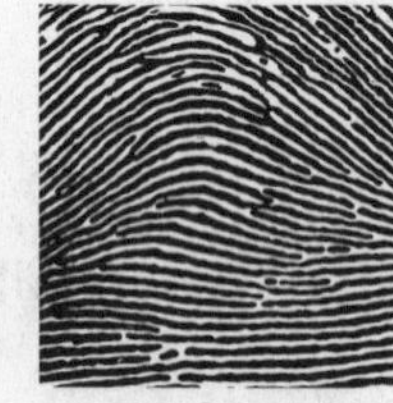

Plain Arch

Common features of fingerprints

LIFE SCIENCE

◆ Skills Objectives

- Observing

◆ Using the QX3 Microscope you Will...

Capture images of your own fingerprints and identify their characteristics.

◆ Materials

QX3 microscope
plain white paper
ink pad

◆ Safety Tips   *Review the safety guidelines in the front of your lab book.*

◆ Procedure

1. Label a sheet of paper with your name. Then roll one of your fingers from side to side on an ink pad. Make a fingerprint by carefully rolling your inked finger from side to side on the paper. Examine your fingerprint using the QX3 microscope. Try to identify some of the characteristics in your fingerprint that are shown in the illustration. Take a snapshot.

Name ____________________ Date __________ Class __________

WHAT DO FINGERPRINTS REVEAL? *(continued)*

2. Divide into groups. Each group should choose one member to use the same finger to make a second fingerprint on a sheet of paper. Leave the paper unlabeled.
3. Exchange your group's fingerprints with those from another group. Compare each labeled fingerprint with the fingerprint on the unlabeled paper. Decide whose fingerprint it is.
4. Wash your hands after completing this activity.

◆ Data Collection and Observations

Record your observations in the space below.

Features present in my fingerprint:

____

____

Features present in the "unknown" fingerprint:

____

____

Identity of the "unknown" fingerprint:

____

____

◆ Analyze and Conclude

1. Why are fingerprints a useful tool for identifying people?

____

____

◆ Going Further

Create a poster that shows the three features (arch, loop, whorl) present in human fingerprints.

LIFE SCIENCE

Name ______________________ Date __________ Class ______________

L8 DISCOVER

How Do Living Things Vary?

◆ Background

As you learned in your study of genetics, members of a species differ from one another in many of their traits. Any difference between individuals of the same species is called variation. For example, some newly hatched turtles are able to swim faster than other turtles. Darwin observed that some variations make individuals better adapted to their environment. Those individuals are more likely to survive and reproduce. When they do reproduce, their offspring may inherit the allele for the helpful trait.

◆ Skills Objective

- Classifying

LIFE SCIENCE

◆ Using the QX3 Microscope you Will...

Capture images of very similar objects, such as sunflower seeds, to show their microscopic variation.

◆ Materials

QX3 microscope
10 sunflower seeds
metric ruler

◆ Safety Tip

Review the safety guidelines in the front of your lab book.

◆ Procedure

1. Use a metric ruler to measure the length and width of 10 sunflower seeds. Record each measurement. Place each seed in a line after you measure it so that the seeds can be examined again in order.
2. Now use the QX3 microscope to carefully examine each seed. Record each seed's shape, color, and number of stripes. Take a snapshot of each seed.

Name ______________________ Date ____________ Class ______________

HOW DO LIVING THINGS VARY? *(continued)*

◆ Data Collection and Observations

Seed #	Length	Width	Shape	Color	Stripes
1					
2					
3					
4					
5					
6					
7					
8					
9					
10					

◆ Analyze and Conclude

1. In what ways are the seeds in your sample different from one another? In what ways are they similar?

____

____

2. How could you group the seeds based on their similarities and differences?

____

____

◆ Going Further

Create a poster or a slide show illustrating the tiny differences you found between sunflower seeds.

LIFE SCIENCE

Name ______________________ Date __________ Class __________

L9 TRY THIS

Feeding Paramecia

◆ Background

Members of one group of protozoans have structures called cilia that they use to move and obtain food. Cilia are hairlike projections from cells that move with a wavelike pattern. Cilia move an organism by acting something like tiny oars. Their movement also sweeps food into the organism. One type of protozoan with cilia is the paramecium.

◆ Skills Objective

You will be able to:

- infer that paramecia are heterotrophs because they ingest the *chlorella* and *chlorella* behave like autotrophs because they do not seem to be ingesting food and are green like plants.

LIFE SCIENCE

◆ Using the QX3 Microscope you Will...

Make a movie of paramecium feeding on a plant-like protist, *chlorella.*

◆ Materials

QX3 microscope
Chlorella culture
paramecium culture
plastic dropper
microscope slide
cotton fibers
colored pencils

◆ Safety Tips

   *Review the safety guidelines in the front of your lab book.*

◆ Procedure

1. Use a plastic dropper to place one drop of paramecium culture on a microscope slide. Add some cotton fibers to slow down the paramecia.
2. Set the QX3 microscope at 10X magnification to find some paramecia.
3. Add one drop of *chlorella* to the paramecium culture on your slide.
4. Switch to 60X magnification, and begin recording a real-time movie. Observe what happens. Using colored pencils, make a drawing in the Data Collection and Observations section of a paramecium that has fed on some *chlorella* cells. Then wash your hands.

Name ______________________ Date __________ Class ______________

FEEDING PARAMECIA *(continued)*

◆ Data Collection and Observations

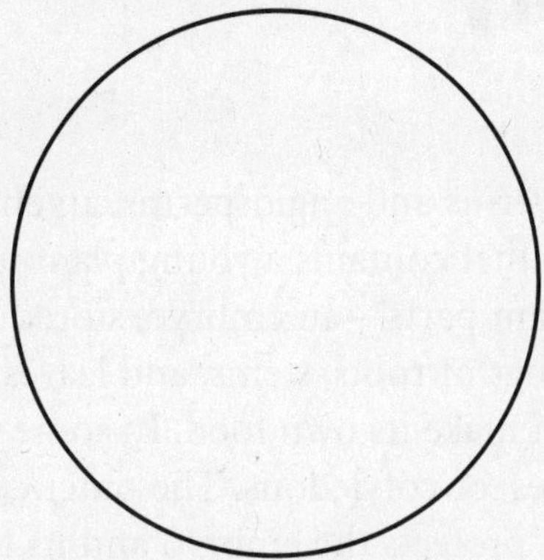

Paramecium feeding, 60X

◆ Analyze and Conclude

1. What evidence do you have that paramecia are heterotrophs?

____

____

2. What evidence do you have that *chlorella* are autotrophs?

____

____

◆ Going Further

Make a time-lapse movie of paramecium feeding over an hour. Set the interval to one minute between frames. At the end of the hour, review the images to find out how many *Chlorella* each paramecium ate.

Name ______________________ Date __________ Class __________

L10 **TRY THIS**

The In-Seed Story

◆ Background

In seed plants, including gymnosperms and angiosperms, an embryo develops inside a seed. A seed is a structure that contains a young plant inside a protective covering. A seed has three important parts—an embryo, stored food, and a seed coat. The embryo has the beginnings of roots, stems, and leaves. The embryo uses food stored in the seed until it can make its own food. In some plants, food is stored inside one or two seed leaves, or cotyledons. The outer covering of a seed is called the seed coat. The seed coat protects the embryo and its food and keeps them from drying out.

LIFE SCIENCE

◆ Skills Objective

You will be able to:

- observe and describe the functions of the cotyledon, seed coat, and the embryo.

◆ Using the QX3 Microscope you Will...

Capture images of the parts of a seed, and label each part.
Measure the sizes of various seeds and seed parts.

◆ Materials

QX3 microscope
dried kidney, lima, or black bean
dried yellow or green pea
clear plastic metric ruler

◆ Safety Tip  *Review the safety guidelines in the front of your lab book.*

◆ Procedure

Your teacher will give you a few different seeds that have been soaked in water.

1. Carefully observe the outside of each seed using the QX3 microscope at 10X magnification. Take a snapshot.
2. Gently remove the coverings of the seeds. Then carefully separate the parts of each seed. Examine the inside of each seed using the QX3 microscope at 10X magnification. Take a snapshot of each seed.
3. Lay the metric ruler down next to the seed on the QX3 microscope stage platform. Measure the length of each seed. Measure the length of each embryo. Record these measurements in the Data Collection and Observations section.
4. Label each of the snapshots with the type of seed and its parts.

THE IN-SEED STORY *(continued)*

◆ Data Collection and Observations

Seed Type	Seed Length *(mm)*	Embryo length *(mm)*

◆ Analyze and Conclude

1. What is the function of the cotyledon?

2. What is the function of the seed coat?

3. What is the function of the embryo?

◆ Going Further

The class can bring in seeds from home—from a garden, dry seeds to be used in cooking, flower seeds, etc. After soaking seeds of each type in water overnight, examine them and try to determine the number of cotyledons they each have. Be sure to take a snapshot of each type of seed, and label it with the appropriate seed part labels and the type of seed that it is. These snapshots can be assembled into a wall mural.

Name ______________________ Date __________ Class __________

L11 SKILLS LAB

Which Way Is Up?

◆ Background

A plant's growth response toward or away from a stimulus is called a tropism. If a plant grows toward the stimulus, it shows a positive tropism. If a plant grows away from a stimulus, it shows a negative tropism. Plants respond to three important external stimuli: touch, light, and gravity. For example, the stems of many vines, such as grapes and morning glories, respond positively to touch. All plants grow toward light, which is a positive tropism. The parts of plants respond differently to gravity. Roots grow downward, which is a positive tropism. However, stems grow upward, which is a negative tropism to gravity.

LIFE SCIENCE

◆ Skills Objective

You will be able to:

- develop hypotheses to explain how the growth of a seed is affected by gravity.

◆ Using the QX3 Microscope you Will...

Make a slide show of embryonic root and stem growth in plants and their response to gravity.

◆ Materials

4 soaked corn seeds
paper towels
water
marking pencil
plastic petri dish
scissors
masking tape
clay

◆ Safety Tip

Review the safety guidelines in the front of your lab book.

◆ Procedure

1. Read over the entire procedure. Then, with your group, develop a hypothesis about the direction in which the seedlings will grow in response to gravity.
2. Arrange four seeds that have been soaked in water for 24 hours in a petri dish. The pointed ends of the seeds should face the center of the dish, as shown in the illustration.

WHICH WAY IS UP? *(continued)*

3. Place a circle cut from paper towel over the seeds. Moisten one or more paper towels with water so that they are wet, but not dripping. Pack them in the dish to hold the seeds firmly in place. Cover the dish, and seal it with tape.
4. Lay the dish upside-down so the seeds show. Use a marking pencil to draw a small, outward-facing arrow over one of the seeds, as shown in the illustration. Turn the dish over, and write your name and the date on it.

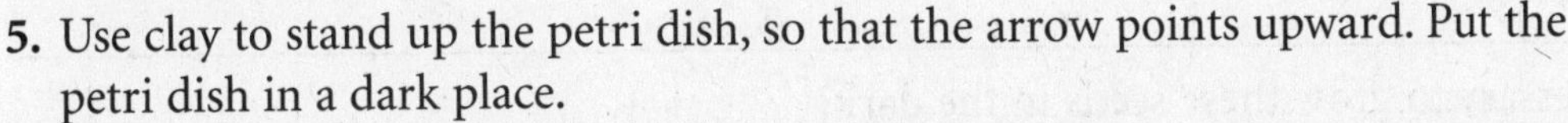

5. Use clay to stand up the petri dish, so that the arrow points upward. Put the petri dish in a dark place.
6. Once a day for a week, remove the petri dish, and check it. Do not open the dish. Observe and sketch the seeds. Note the seeds' direction of growth. Take a snapshot of the seeds' growth with the QX3 microscope. Then, return the dish, making sure that the arrow points upward.

◆ Data Collection and Observations

Day	Observations/Notes
1	
2	
3	
4	
5	
6	
7	

WHICH WAY IS UP? *(continued)*

◆ Analyze and Conclude

1. What new structures emerged as the seeds developed? How did the direction of growth compare from seed to seed?

2. Did your results confirm your hypothesis? If not, describe any differences between your hypothesis and your results.

3. Why was it necessary to grow these seeds in the dark?

4. What evidence or ideas did you consider when you wrote your hypothesis? Did any of your ideas change as a result of this experiment? Explain.

◆ Going Further

Make a time-lapse movie to determine if seedlings grow in response to the direction of light. Plant some beans in soil in a small container, and water them well. The soil should be very wet, but not have standing water on top of the soil. Place the container in a dark place, and check it daily. As soon as you see shoots beginning to emerge from the soil, place a flexible lamp parallel with the side of the container at the level of the counter, and turn it on, so that the light shines on the container from the side. There should not be another light source in the room, so that the seedlings are exposed to a strong directional light. Prop the QX3 microscope next to the light source, bracing it as you did before. Record a time-lapse movie set at one-hour intervals. Compare your results with the seeds' response to gravity.

Name ____________________ Date __________ Class __________

L12 **DISCOVER**

How Do Natural and Synthetic Sponges Compare?

◆ Background

You might use a brightly colored synthetic sponge to mop up a spill. That sponge is filled with holes, and so are the animals called sponges. The body of a sponge is something like a bag that is pierced all over with openings, called pores. The pores are important in functions, such as reproducing, and obtaining food and oxygen. Most sponges have irregular shapes without symmetry. While some of their cells do specialized jobs, sponges lack the tissues and organs that most other animals have.

◆ Skills Objective

You will be able to:

- observe similarities and differences between natural and synthetic sponges.

◆ Using the QX3 Microscope you Will...

Capture images of synthetic and natural sponges for comparison.

◆ Materials

natural sponges
synthetic kitchen sponges
scissors
QX3 microscope

◆ Safety Tips   *Review the safety guidelines in the front of your lab book.*

◆ Procedure

1. Examine a natural sponge, and then use the QX3 microscope at 10X magnification to take a closer look at its surface. Look carefully at the holes in the sponge. Draw what you see in the Data Collection and Observations section. Take a snapshot.
2. Cut out a small piece of sponge, and examine it with the QX3 microscope at 60X magnification. Draw what you see in the Data Collection and Observations section.
3. Repeat Steps 1 and 2 with a synthetic kitchen sponge.

LIFE SCIENCE

Name ______________________ Date __________ Class ______________

◆ Data Collection and Observations

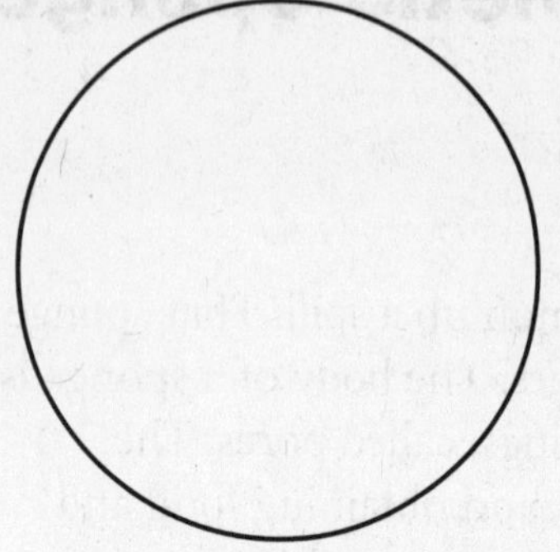

Natural sponge, 10X

Natural sponge, 60X

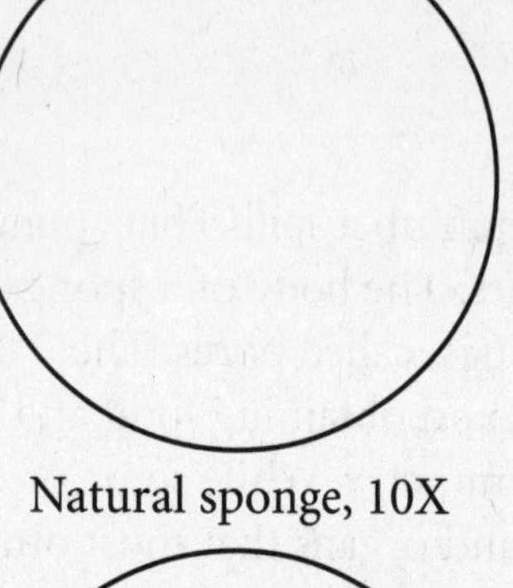

Synthetic sponge, 10X

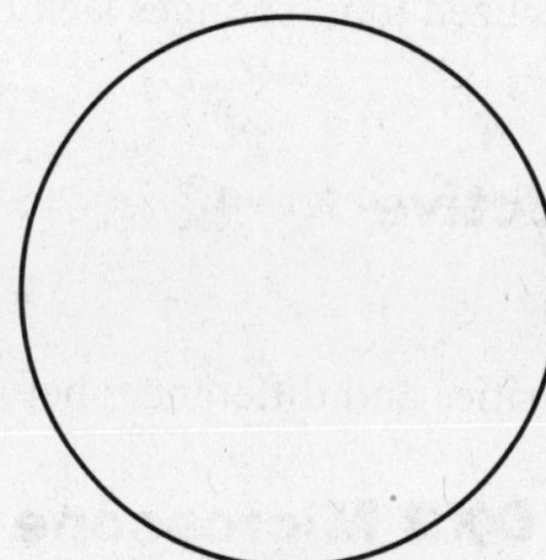

Synthetic sponge, 60X

◆ Analyze and Conclude

1. What are three ways that natural and synthetic sponges are similar?

____

____

2. What are three ways that natural and synthetic sponges are different?

____

____

____

◆ Going Further

Create a poster showing the three types of similarities and three types of differences between natural and synthetic sponges using the snapshots you took with the QX3 microscope.

Name ______________________ Date __________ Class ______________

L13 **TRY THIS**

Hydra Doing?

◆ Background

Jellyfish, sea anemones, hydras, and corals are cnidarians. Cnidarians are soft-bodied, radially symmetrical invertebrates that have long, wavy tentacles arranged around an opening, called a mouth. The tentacles are covered with stinging cells. Cnidarians are carnivores that use stinging cells to capture their prey and to defend themselves. Cnidarians reproduce both sexually and asexually.

◆ Skills Objective

You will be able to:

- observe the movement and feeding behavior of hydra.

◆ Using the QX3 Microscope you Will...

Make a movie of movement in hydra.

◆ Materials

QX3 microscope
small bowl or petri dish
toothpicks
live hydra

◆ Safety Tips   

Review the safety guidelines in the front of your lab book.

◆ Procedure

1. Put a drop of water that contains hydras in a small unbreakable bowl or petri dish. Allow it to sit for about 15 minutes.
2. Use the QX3 microscope to examine the hydras as they move about. Make a short real-time movie of their movements. Continue recording while you gently touch the tentacles of the hydra with the end of a toothpick. Watch what happens.
3. Return the hydras to your teacher, and wash your hands.

LIFE SCIENCE

Name ______________________ Date __________ Class ______________

◆ Data Collection and Observations

Action	Observations/Notes
Normal movement	
After touching tentacles	

LIFE SCIENCE

◆ Analyze and Conclude

1. Describe a hydra's method of movement.

____

____

◆ Going Further

If a culture of small, water fleas (*Daphnia*) is available, use a plastic dropper to add a couple to the water drop containing the hydras. Use the QX3 microscope to record a movie of the feeding behavior of hydra.

Name ______________________ Date __________ Class ______________

L14 **DISCOVER**

What Are Feathers Like?

◆ Background

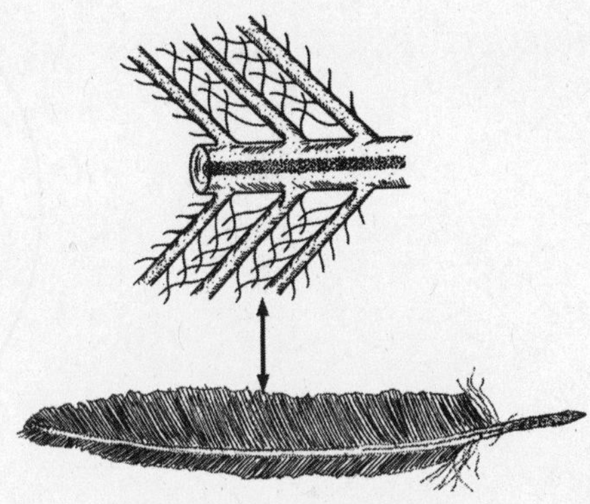

Feather structure

Feathers are a major structural adaptation that enable birds to fly. Birds have different types of feathers. A contour feather is one of the large feathers that give shape to a bird's body. When a bird flies, these feathers help it balance and steer. In addition to contour feathers, birds have short, soft, fluffy down feathers next to the skin. Down feathers function to trap heat and keep the bird warm. In effect, down feathers cover a bird in lightweight long underwear.

LIFE SCIENCE

◆ Skills

You will be able to:

- observe feathers and their components.

◆ Using the QX3 Microscope you Will...

Capture images of different feathers and their components.

◆ Materials

QX3 microscope
feathers

◆ Safety Tips

   *Review the safety guidelines in the front of your lab book.*

◆ Procedure

1. Examine a feather. Observe its overall shape and structure. Use the QX3 microscope at 10X magnification to examine the many hairlike barbs that project out from the feather's central shaft. Take a snapshot.
2. With your fingertip, gently stroke the feather from bottom to top. Observe whether the barbs stick together or separate. Take a snapshot.
3. Gently separate two barbs in the middle of the feather. Rub the separated edges with your fingertip.
4. Use the QX3 microscope to examine the feather, including the edges of the two separated barbs. Switch to 60X magnification and examine this area again. Draw a diagram of what you observe.
5. Now rejoin the two separated barbs by gently pulling outward from the shaft. Then wash your hands.

Name ______________________ Date __________ Class __________

◆ Data Collection and Observations

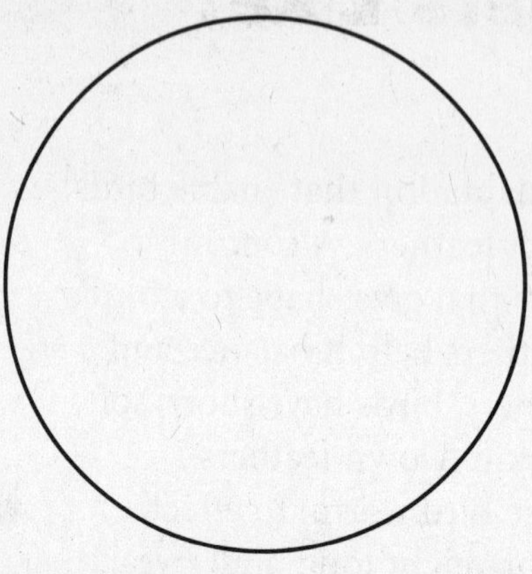

Feather, 60X

◆ Analyze and Conclude

1. Once barbs have been separated, is it easy to rejoin them?

____

____

2. How might the rejoining of barbs be an advantage to the bird?

____

____

◆ Going Further

The class can construct a poster of images of feathers from different types of birds. Be sure to label each image with the type of feather, the bird it came from, and the function of this feather type.

Name ______________________ Date __________ Class ______________

L15 **SKILLS LAB**

Looking at an Owl's Leftovers

◆ Background

An interaction in which one organism hunts and kills another for food is called predation. The organism that does the killing is the predator. The organism that is caught is the prey. Predator-prey relationships are one way in which organisms interact in an ecosystem. All owls are predators. They feed on various kinds of prey. In this lab you will gather evidence and draw conclusions about an owl's diet.

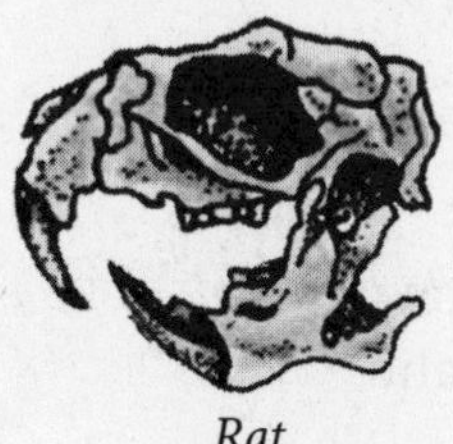
Rat

Vole

Mouse

Shrew

Mole

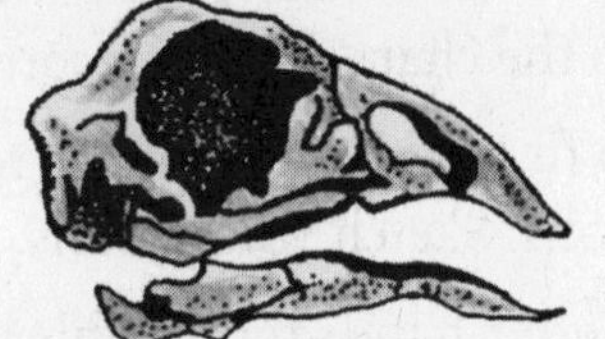
Small bird

LIFE SCIENCE

◆ Skills Objective

You will be able to:

- draw conclusions about the diet of owls by studying the pellets they cough up.

◆ Using the QX3 Microscope You Will...

Create poster images of various prey item remains from owl pellets.

◆ Materials

QX3 microscope
owl pellet
dissecting needle
forceps
metric ruler

◆ Safety Tips

Review the safety guidelines in the front of your lab book.

Name ______________________ Date __________ Class __________

LOOKING AT AN OWL'S LEFTOVERS *(continued)*

◆ Procedure

1. An owl pellet is a collection of undigested materials that an owl coughs up after a meal. Write a hypothesis describing what items you expect an owl pellet to contain. List the reasons for your hypothesis.
2. Use the QX3 microscope to observe the outside of an owl pellet. Take a snapshot. Record your observations.
3. Use one hand to grasp the owl pellet with forceps. Hold a dissecting needle in your other hand, and use it to gently separate the pellet into pieces. **CAUTION:** *Dissecting needles are sharp. Never cut material toward you; always cut away from your body.*
4. Using the forceps and dissecting needle, carefully separate the bones from the rest of the pellet. Remove any fur that night be attached to bones.
5. Group similar bones together in separate piles. Observe the skulls, and draw them. Record the number of skulls, their length, and the number, shape, and color of the teeth. Take snapshots of each of the bones.
6. Use the chart to determine what kinds of skulls you found. If any skulls do not match the chart exactly, record which animal each skull resembles most.
7. Try to fit together any of the remaining bones to form complete or partial skeletons. Sketch your results.
8. Wash your hands thoroughly with soap and water when you are finished.

LIFE SCIENCE

◆ Data Collection and Observations

Record your observations in the space below.

Items expected to be found in an owl pellet (hypothesis):

____

____

Reasons for this hypothesis:

____

____

Observations about the outside of an owl pellet

Name ______________________ Date ____________ Class ______________

LOOKING AT AN OWL'S LEFTOVERS *(continued)*

Items in owl pellet	Types of bones	Notes

◆ Analyze and Conclude

1. How many animals' remains were in the pellet? What data led you to that conclusion?

____

____

2. Combine your results with those of your classmates. Which three animals were eaten most frequently? How do these results compare to your hypothesis?

____

____

3. Owls cough up about two pellets a day. Based on your class's data, what can you predict about the number of animals an owl might eat in one month?

____

____

4. In this lab, you were able to examine only the part of the owl's diet that it did not digest. How might this fact affect your confidence in the conclusions you reached?

____

____

◆ Going Further

Create poster images of the skulls or partial or complete skeletons of the prey items that you found in the owl pellet. Label each with the identity of the animal eaten as food by the owl.

LIFE SCIENCE

Name ______________________ Date __________ Class ______________

L16 REAL WORLD LAB

One for All

◆ Background

Some animals, including ants, termites, honeybees, naked mole rats, and pistol shrimp live in groups, called societies. A society is a group of closely related animals of the same species that work together for the benefit of the whole group. Different members perform specific tasks, such as gathering food or caring for young. The behavior of animals is instinctive and rigid—an animal in a society is "preprogrammed" to perform a specific job.

◆ Skills Objectives

LIFE SCIENCE

You will be able to:

- observe ants perform several different tasks;
- infer the division of labor in an ant colony.

◆ Using the QX3 Microscope you Will...

Make a movie of the daily activities of a portion of an ant colony.
Capture images of ant anatomy.

◆ Materials

QX3 microscope
large glass jar
wire screen
sugar
20-30 large, black ants
large, thick rubber band
forceps
sandy soil
bread crumbs
black paper
shallow pan
sponge
wax pencil
tape

◆ Safety Tips

Review the safety guidelines in the front of your lab book.

Name ______________________ Date __________ Class ______________

ONE FOR ALL *(continued)*

◆ Procedure

1. Read over the entire lab to preview the kinds of observations you will be making.
2. Mark a large jar with four evenly spaced vertical lines. Label the sections A, B, C, and D.
3. Fill the jar about three-fourths full with soil. Place the jar in a shallow pan of water to prevent any ants from escaping. Place a wet sponge in the jar as a water source.
4. Observe the condition of the soil, both on the surface and along the sides of the jar. Record your observations for each section in the Data Collection and Observations section.
5. Add the ants to the jar. **CAUTION:** *Do not use fire ants. Immediately cover the jar with the wire screen, using the rubber band to hold the screen firmly in place.*
6. Observe the ants for 10 minutes. Use the QX3 microscope to take snapshots of individual ants. Look for differences among the adult ants. Look for eggs, larvae, and pupae. Examine both individual behavior and interactions. Make short movies of behaviors and interactions using the QX3 microscope.
7. Remove the screen, and add some bread crumbs and sugar to the jar. Close the cover. Observe the response to the stimulus for 10 more minutes. Take snapshots and make short movies documenting the ants' behaviors.
8. Wrap black paper around the jar above the water line. Remove the paper only when making your observations.
9. Observe the ants every day for two weeks. Take new snapshots or movies to add to your collection whenever you observe new individuals or behaviors. Look at the soil, and examine the food. If any food is moldy, use forceps to remove it. Place the moldy food in a plastic bag, seal the bag, and throw it away. Add more food as necessary, and keep the sponge moist. When you finish your observations, replace the paper.

LIFE SCIENCE

Name ______________________ Date __________ Class ______________

ONE FOR ALL *(continued)*

◆ Data Collection and Observations

Soil Condition Before Adding Ants		
Section	Soil Condition at Surface	Soil Condition along Sides
A		
B		
C		
D		

Soil Condition Before Adding Ants		
Section	Soil Condition at Surface	Soil Condition along Sides
A		
B		
C		
D		

LIFE SCIENCE

◆ Analyze and Conclude

1. Describe the various types of ants you saw. What evidence, if any, did you observe that different kinds of ants perform different tasks?

____

____

2. How do the different behaviors you observed contribute to the survival of the colony?

____

____

3. How did the soil change over the period of your observations? What caused those changes? How do you know?

____

____

4. Based on this lab, what kinds of environmental conditions do you think ant colonies need to thrive outdoors?

____

____

◆ Going Further

Put together a slide show that illustrates an ant society. Show life history examples, such as eggs, larvae, pupae, workers, larger workers or "soldiers." Create movies that illustrate how ants communicate with each other.

Name ______________________ Date __________ Class ______________

L17 **DISCOVER**

Hard as a Rock?

◆ Background

The femur, or thighbone, connects the pelvic bones to the lower leg bones. Notice that a thin, tough membrane covers all of the bone except the ends. Blood vessels and nerves enter and leave the bone through the membrane. Beneath the membrane is a layer of compact bone, which is dense, but not solid. Small canals run through the compact bone. These canals carry blood vessels and nerves from the bone's surface to the living cells within the bone. Just inside the compact bone is a layer of spongy bone. Spongy bone is also found at the ends of the bone. Although spongy bone has many small spaces like a sponge, it is hard like all bones. This structure functions to make spongy bone lightweight but strong.

LIFE SCIENCE

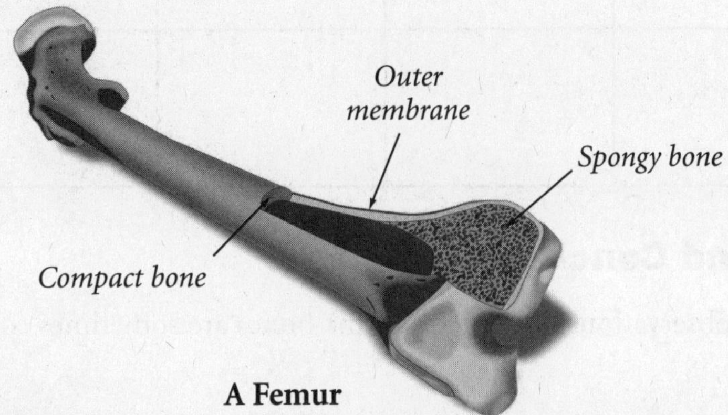

A Femur

◆ Skills Objective

- Observing

◆ Using the QX3 Microscope you Will...

Capture images of the external surfaces of rocks and bones.

◆ Materials

QX3 microscope
leg bone from a cooked chicken or turkey
rock of similar size as leg bone

◆ Safety Tips  *Review the safety guidelines in the front of your lab book.*

◆ Procedure

1. Your teacher will give you a leg bone from a cooked turkey or chicken and a rock.

Name ______________________ Date __________ Class __________

HARD AS A ROCK? *(continued)*

2. Use the QX3 microscope to examine both the rock and the bone. Take snapshots of each.
3. Gently tap both the rock and the bone on a hard surface.
4. Pick up each object to feel how heavy it is.
5. Wash your hands. Then make notes of your observations in the Data and Observations section.

◆ Data Collection and Observations

Item	Size/Shape	Texture	Strength	Notes
Bone				
Rock				

LIFE SCIENCE

◆ Analyze and Conclude

1. Based on your observations, why do you think bones are sometimes compared to rocks?

____

____

2. List some ways in which bones and rocks are similar and different.

____

____

◆ Going Further

Using the QX3 microscope, examine the internal anatomy of a chicken bone that has been sawed crosswise. Take a snapshot of the bone structure at the cut end of the bone. Construct a poster comparing the external and internal bone structure.

Name ______________________ Date __________ Class ______________

L18 **SKILLS LAB**

A Look Beneath the Skin

◆ Background

Some of your body's movements, such as smiling, are easy to control. Other movements, such as the beating of your heart, are impossible to control completely. That is because some muscles are not under your conscious control. Those muscles are called involuntary muscles. Involuntary muscles are responsible for activities, such as breathing and digesting food. The muscles that are under your control are called voluntary muscles. Smiling, turning a page in a book, and getting out of your chair when the bell rings are all actions controlled by voluntary muscles.

◆ Skills Objectives

You will be able to:

- observe the structure and function of the muscles in a chicken wing;
- classify the muscles based on their observations.

◆ Using the QX3 Microscope you Will...

Capture microscopic images of tendons, ligaments, muscles, and bones.

◆ Materials

QX3 microscope
protective gloves
paper towels
dissecting scissors
water
dissection tray
uncooked chicken wing, treated with bleach

◆ Safety Tips

Review the safety guidelines in the front of your lab book.

◆ Procedure

1. Work in pairs. One member of the pair should put on protective gloves. **CAUTION:** *Wear gloves whenever you handle the chicken.* The other member of the pair will use the QX3 microscope to capture images of the wing's structures.
2. Your teacher will give you a chicken wing. Rinse it well with water, dry it with paper towels, and place it in a dissecting tray.

LIFE SCIENCE

Name ______________________ Date __________ Class ______________

A LOOK BENEATH THE SKIN *(continued)*

3. Carefully extend the wing. Hold the wing extended while your lab partner draws a diagram of the external structure. Label the upper arm, elbow, lower arm, and hand (wing tip).

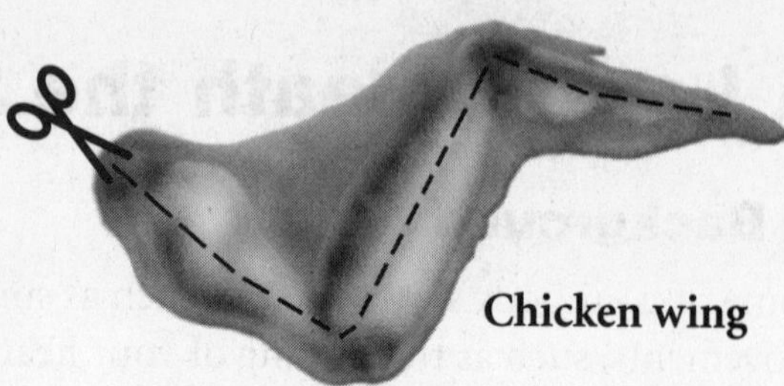

4. Use scissors to remove the skin. Cut along the cut line as shown in the illustration. **CAUTION:** *Cut away from your body and your classmates.*
5. Examine the muscles, the bundles of pink tissue around the bones. Find two groups of muscles in the upper arm. Hold the arm down at the shoulder, and alternately pull on each muscle group. Observe what happens. Your lab partner should take a hand-held snapshot of muscle tissue with the QX3 microscope.
6. Find the two groups of muscles in the lower arm. Hold down the arm at the elbow, and alternately pull on each muscle group. Then, your partner should make a diagram of the wing's muscles.
7. Find the tendons—shiny white tissue at the ends of muscles. Notice what parts the tendons connect. Add the tendons to your diagram, and take a snapshot of a tendon with the QX3 microscope.
8. Remove the muscles and tendons. Find the ligaments, the whitish, ribbonlike structures between bones. Add them to your diagram, and take a snapshot of a ligament with the QX3 microscope.
9. Dispose of the chicken parts according to your teacher's instructions. Wash your hands.

◆ Data Collection and Observations

Record your observations in the space below.

Sketch chicken wing muscles, tendons, and ligaments.

LIFE SCIENCE

Name ______________________ Date __________ Class ______________

A LOOK BENEATH THE SKIN *(continued)*

◆ Analyze and Conclude

1. How does a chicken wing move at the elbow? How does the motion compare to how your elbow moves? What type of joint is involved?

____

____

2. What happened when you pulled on one of the arm muscles? What muscle action does the pulling represent?

____

____

3. Classify the muscles you observed as smooth, cardiac, or skeletal.

____

____

4. Why is it valuable to record your observations with accurate diagrams and snapshots?

____

____

◆ Going Further

Create a poster showing the different types of structures found in the limb of a chicken. Be sure to label all the structures appropriately, with their name, as well as their function.

LIFE SCIENCE

Name ______________________ Date __________ Class ______________

L19 **DISCOVER**

What Can You Observe About Skin?

◆ Background

The skin performs several major functions in the body. The skin covers the body and prevents the loss of water. It protects the body from injury and infection. The skin also helps to regulate body temperature, eliminate wastes, gather information about the environment, and produce vitamin D. Skin protects the body by forming a barrier that keeps disease-causing microorganisms and harmful substances outside the body. In addition, the skin helps keep important substances inside the body. Like plastic wrap that keeps food from drying out, the skin prevents the loss of important fluids such as water.

LIFE SCIENCE

◆ Skills Objective

- Inferring

◆ Using the QX3 Microscope you Will...

Capture images of your own skin's structure.

◆ Materials

QX3 microscope
plastic gloves

◆ Safety Tip

Review the safety guidelines in the front of your lab book.

◆ Procedure

1. Using the QX3 microscope in hand-held mode, examine the skin on your hand. Look for pores and hairs on both the palm and the back of your hand. Take snapshots of any features you see. Record your observations in the Data and Observations section.
2. Place a plastic glove on your hand. After five minutes, remove the glove. Then examine the skin on your hand with the QX3 microscope. Take another snapshot. Record your observations in the Data and Observations section.

Name _______________ Date _______ Class _______

WHAT CAN YOU OBSERVE ABOUT SKIN? *(continued)*

◆ Data Collection and Observations

Treatment	Observations
Hand without glove	
Hand with glove	

◆ Analyze and Conclude

1. Compare your hand before and after wearing the glove.

2. What happened to the skin when you wore the glove? Why did this happen?

◆ Going Further

Create a poster showing the structures found in the skin, such as hairs, freckles, sweat pores, and fingerprints.

LIFE SCIENCE

Name ______________________ Date __________ Class ______________

L20 **SHARPEN YOUR SKILLS**

Predicting the Presence of Starch

◆ Background

Simple carbohydrates are also known as sugars. There are many types of sugars. They are found naturally in fruits, milk, and some vegetables. One sugar, glucose, is the major source of energy for your body's cells. Complex carbohydrates are made up of many sugar molecules linked together in a chain. Starch is a complex carbohydrate found in plant foods such as potatoes, rice, corn, and grain products, such as pasta, cereals, and bread. To use starch as an energy source, your body first breaks it down into smaller, individual sugar molecules. These sugar molecules are then involved in chemical reactions where energy is produced.

LIFE SCIENCE

◆ Skills Objective

- Predicting

◆ Using the QX3 Microscope you Will...

Capture images of starchy and nonstarchy foods before and after application of iodine (a starch indicator solution).

◆ Materials

QX3 microscope
selection of foods such as fruits, vegetables, rice, bread, cereal, and soft drinks
iodine solution
plastic dropper
test tubes
notebook
microscope slide

◆ Safety Tips    *Review the safety guidelines in the front of your lab book.*

◆ Procedure

1. Obtain food samples from your teacher. Write a prediction stating whether each food contains starch. Then test your predictions.
2. First, put on your apron. Then use a plastic dropper to add three drops of iodine to each food sample. If the iodine turns blue-black, starch is present. **CAUTION:** *Iodine can stain skin and clothing. Handle it carefully.*
3. Choose a vegetable that turned blue-black and place a small, thin piece of that food on a microscope slide. Examine it with the QX3 microscope. Take a snapshot.

Name ______________________ Date __________ Class __________

PREDICTING THE PRESENCE OF STARCH *(continued)*

4. Now add three drops of iodine at one edge of the vegetable on the slide and observe what happens as the iodine comes in contact with it. Take another snapshot.

◆ Data Collection and Observations

Food	Prediction

◆ Analyze and Conclude

1. Which foods contain starch?

____

____

◆ Going Further

Create a poster of several different types of starchy foods before and after the iodine starch test.

LIFE SCIENCE

Name ______________________ Date __________ Class ______________

L21 DISCOVER

What Kinds of Cells are in Blood?

◆ Background

If someone fills a test tube with blood and lets it sit for a while, the blood separates into layers. The top layer is a clear, yellowish liquid. A dark red material rests on the bottom. The top layer is plasma, which is the liquid part of blood. The red material at the bottom is a mixture of blood cells. Blood is made up of four components: plasma, red blood cells, white blood cells, and platelets. About 45 percent of the volume of blood is made up of cells. The rest consists of plasma.

◆ Skills Objective

- Observing

LIFE SCIENCE

◆ Using the QX3 Microscope you Will...

Capture images of the components of blood.

◆ Materials

QX3 microscope
prepared slide of human blood

◆ Safety Tips

  *Review the safety guidelines in the front of your lab book.*

◆ Procedure

1. Obtain a microscope slide of human blood from your teacher. Look at the slide under the QX3 microscope, first at 60X, and then at 200X magnification.
2. Look carefully at the different kinds of cells that you see.
3. Make several drawings of each kind of cell in the Data Collection and Observations section. Use a red pencil for the blood cells. Take snapshots of each of the blood components.

Name ______________________ Date __________ Class ______________

WHAT KINDS OF CELLS ARE IN BLOOD? *(continued)*

◆ Data Collection and Observations

Record your observations in the space below.

Red Blood Cells

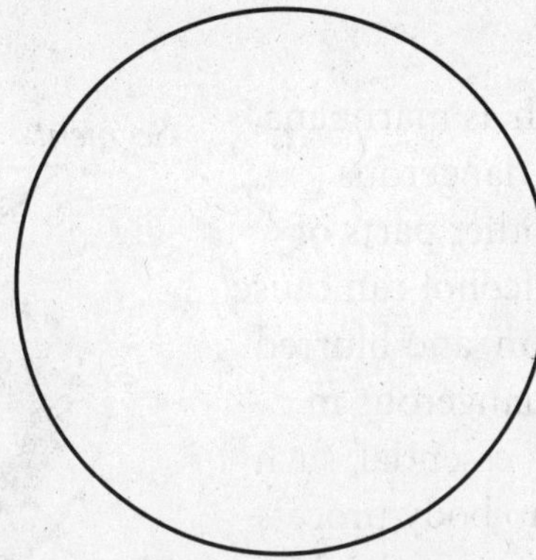

White Blood Cells

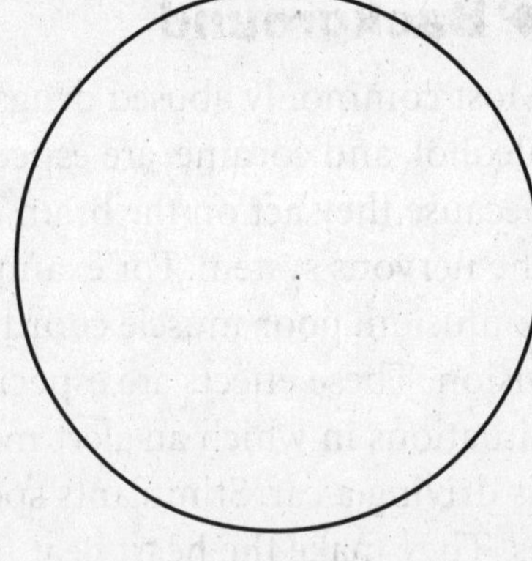

Platelets

LIFE SCIENCE

◆ Analyze and Conclude

1. How many kinds of cells did you see? How do they differ from one another?

____

____

◆ Going Further

Create a poster showing the different cell types in human blood, labeled with their names and functions.

Name ______________________ Date __________ Class __________

L22 REAL WORLD LAB

With Caffeine or Without?

◆ Background

Most commonly abused drugs, such as marijuana, alcohol, and cocaine, are especially dangerous because they act on the brain and other parts of the nervous system. For example, alcohol can cause confusion, poor muscle coordination, and blurred vision. These effects are especially dangerous in situations in which an alert mind is essential, such as driving a car. Stimulants speed up body processes. They make the heart beat faster and make the breathing rate increase. Cocaine and nicotine are stimulants, as are amphetamines. Amphetamines are prescription drugs that are sometimes sold illegally.

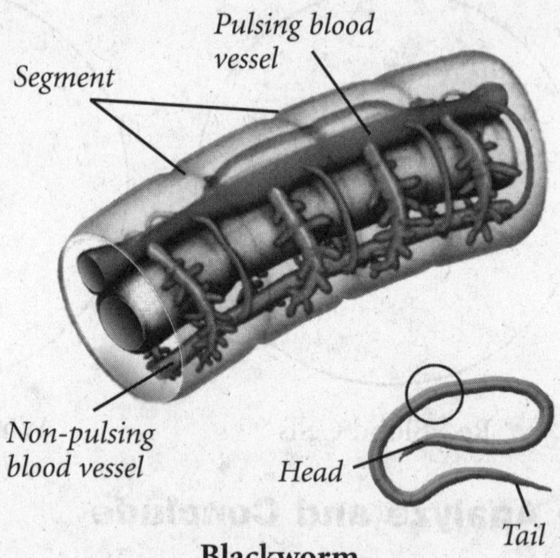

Blackworm

LIFE SCIENCE

◆ Skills Objectives

You will be able to:

- develop hypotheses about the effect of caffeine on an organism;
- design experiments to test their hypotheses.

◆ Using the QX3 Microscope you Will...

Make a movie of the heart rate change in blackworms under different environmental conditions.

◆ Materials

QX3 microscope
blackworms
plastic dropper
paraffin specimen trough
adrenaline solution
non-carbonated spring water
beverages with and without caffeine

◆ Safety Tips   

Review the safety guidelines in the front of your lab book.

Name ______________________ Date __________ Class __________

◆ Procedure

Part 1: Observing Effects of a Known Stimulant

1. Use a dropper to remove one worm and one or two drops of water from a blackworm population provided by your teacher.
2. Place the worm and the water in the trough of the paraffin block. Use the dropper or the corner of a paper towel to remove any excess water that does not fit in the trough. Let the blackworm adjust to the block for a few minutes.
3. Place the paraffin block on the stage platform of the QX3 microscope. Select the lowest amount of light and 10X magnification to view the blackworm.
4. Locate a segment near the middle of the worm. Record a movie of the blood pulses through the segment for 30 seconds. Stop recording and review the movie to determine the number of pulses in 30 seconds. Multiply this number by two to get the pulse in beats per minute. Record the pulse in the Data Collection and Observations section.
5. Remove the block from the microscope. Use the dropper to add one drop of adrenaline solution to the trough. (Adrenaline is a substance that is produced by the human body and acts in a manner similar to a stimulant.) Let the worm sit in the adrenaline solution for five minutes.
6. Place the paraffin block back on the QX3 microscope. Again locate the segment near the middle of the worm. Make another 30-second movie of the worm's pulse. Review the movie to count the pulses, and multiply by two to get the pulse in beats per minute. Record the blackworm's pulse with adrenaline.

Part 2: Testing the Effects of Caffeine

7. Using the procedure you followed in Part 1, design an experiment that tests the effect of caffeine on the blackworm's pulse. You can use beverages with and without caffeine in your investigation. Write a hypothesis and control all necessary variables.
8. Submit your experimental plan to your teacher for review. After making any necessary changes, carry out your experiment.

◆ Data Collection and Observations

Treatment	Blackworm Pulse Rate (30 second count X 2) in beats per minute
Under unstressed conditions	
With adrenaline	
With caffeine	

LIFE SCIENCE

Name ______________ Date ______ Class ______________

WITH CAFFEINE OR WITHOUT? *(continued)*

◆ Analyze and Conclude

1. What effect does a stimulant have on the body?

____

____

2. In Part 1, how did you know that adrenaline acted as a stimulant?

____

____

3. In Part 2, did caffeine act as a stimulant?

____

____

4. Based on your work in Part 2, how do you think your body would react to drinks with caffeine? To drinks without caffeine?

____

____

◆ Going Further

Evaluate the effect of over-the-counter medicines, such as daytime and nighttime cold and cough remedies. Determine if these medicines have a stimulating or depressive effect on the pulse rate of the blackworm. Use a 1mL per 100 mL (water) dilution concentration for evaluation.

LIFE SCIENCE

Name ____________________ Date __________ Class __________

L23 **TRY THIS**

Desert Survival

◆ Background

A desert is an area that receives less than 25 centimeters of rain per year. The amount of evaporation in a desert is greater than the amount of precipitation. Desert organisms are adapted to the lack of rain and to the extreme temperatures. An adaptation is a characteristic that helps an organism survive in its environment and reproduce. For example, the trunk of a saguaro cactus has folds that work like the pleats in an accordion. The trunk of the cactus expands to hold more water when it is raining.

◆ Skills Objective

- Observing

◆ Using the QX3 Microscope you Will...

Capture images of the microscopic anatomy of a cactus.

◆ Materials

QX3 microscope
small potted cactus
scissors

◆ Safety Tips   

Review the safety guidelines in the front of your lab book.

◆ Procedure

1. Use the QX3 microscope in hand-held mode to carefully observe a small potted cactus. Be careful of the spines! Take a few snapshots of the external surfaces of the cactus.
2. With a pair of scissors, carefully snip a small piece from the tip of the cactus.
3. Use the QX3 microscope in hand-held mode to examine the inside of the plant where it was cut. Take snapshots of interesting features. Note any characteristics that seem different from those of other plants.

LIFE SCIENCE

Name ______________________ Date __________ Class __________

DESERT SURVIVAL *(continued)*

◆ Data Collection and Observations

Area	Observations/Notes
External surface of cactus	
Internal structure of cactus	

LIFE SCIENCE

◆ Analyze and Conclude

1. How is the inside of the cactus different from the outside?

____

____

2. Suggest how the features you observe might be related to the desert habitat of the cactus.

____

____

◆ Going Further

Create a poster illustrating the various parts of a cactus, along with labels that describe the function of each part. Can you identify plant organs, such as leaves and stems?

Name ______________________ Date __________ Class __________

L24 **SKILLS LAB**

Change in a Tiny Community

◆ Background

A community is all the different organisms that live together in an area. A community in an ecosystem is in equilibrium, or a state of balance, when the numbers and species of organisms in it do not change suddenly. Events, such as fires, floods, volcanoes, and hurricanes disrupt the equilibrium of a community by changing it drastically in a very short time. But even without a disaster, communities sometimes change. Succession is a series of predictable changes that occur in a community over time. After a fire, volcano, or other disaster, succession enables an ecosystem to recover.

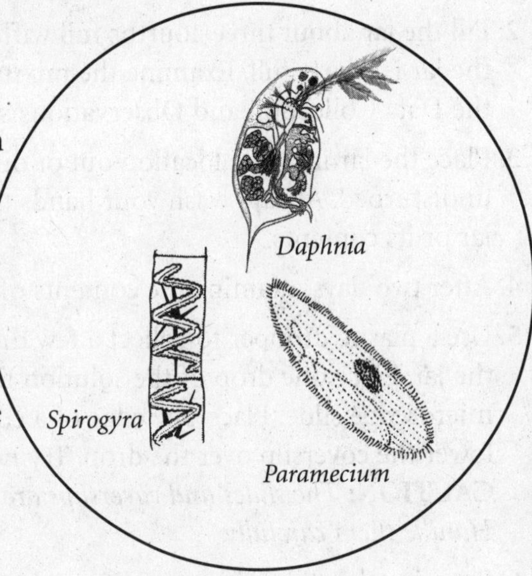

Pond Organisms

◆ Skills Objectives

You will be able to:

- make and observe a model of a microscopic pond community;
- compare and contrast the types of organisms and the sizes of the populations present in the community at intervals;
- conclude that the predominance of various populations changed during the observation period.

◆ Using the QX3 Microscope you Will...

Take snapshots that reflect the diversity of pond life at different time intervals.

◆ Materials

QX3 microscope
hay solution
small baby-food jar
plastic dropper
microscope slide
coverslip
pond water
wax pencil

◆ Safety Tips   

Review the safety guidelines in the front of your lab book.

LIFE SCIENCE

Name _______________ Date _________ Class _______________

CHANGE IN A TINY COMMUNITY *(continued)*

◆ Procedure

1. Use a wax pencil to label a small jar with your name.
2. Fill the jar about three-fourths full with hay solution. Add pond water until the jar is nearly full. Examine the mixture, and record your observations in the Data Collection and Observations section.
3. Place the jar in a safe location out of direct sunlight, where it will remain undisturbed. Always wash your hands thoroughly with soap after handling the jar or its contents.
4. After two days, examine the contents of the jar, and record your observations.
5. Use a plastic dropper to collect a few drops from the surface of the solution in the jar. Place one drop of the solution to be examined in the middle of a microscope slide. Place one edge of a coverslip at the edge of the drop. Gently lower the coverslip over the drop. Try not to trap any air bubbles. **CAUTION:** *The slides and coverslips are fragile, and their edges are sharp. Handle them carefully.*
6. Examine the slide with the QX3 microscope using each magnification (10X, 60X, 200X). Take a snapshot of each type of organism you observe. Estimate the number of each type of organism in your sample.
7. Repeat Steps 5 and 6 with a drop of solution taken from the side of the jar beneath the surface.
8. Repeat Steps 5 and 6 with a drop of solution taken from the bottom of the jar. When you are finished, follow your teacher's directions about cleaning up.
9. After 3 days, repeat Steps 5 through 8.
10. After 3 more days, repeat Steps 5 through 8 again. Then follow your teacher's directions for returning the solution.

Name ______________________ Date __________ Class ______________

CHANGE IN A TINY COMMUNITY *(continued)*

◆ Data Collection and Observations

Day #	Organism Name/Sketch	Location in "Pond" *(top, middle, bottom)*	Number of this Organism Present

◆ Analyze and Conclude

1. Identify as many of the organisms you observed as possible. Use the diagrams in your textbook and any other resources your teacher provides.

LIFE SCIENCE

Name ______________________ Date __________ Class __________

CHANGE IN A TINY COMMUNITY *(continued)*

2. How did the community change over the time that you made your observations?

3. What factors may have influenced the changes in this community?

4. Where did the organisms you observed in the jar come from?

5. Do you think your observations gave you a complete picture of the changes in this community? Explain your answer.

LIFE SCIENCE

◆ Going Further

Design an experiment that would simulate the effect of changing seasons on the "pond." Take snapshots of the changes in the community that occur during these "seasonal" changes.

Name ______________________ Date ____________ Class ______________

L25 **DISCOVER**

How Much Variety is There?

◆ Background

No one knows exactly how many species live on Earth. So far, more than 1.7 million species have been identified. The number of different species in an area is called its biodiversity. It is difficult to estimate the total biodiversity on Earth because many areas of the planet have not been thoroughly studied. Some experts think that the deep oceans alone could contain 10 million new species! Protecting this diversity is a major environmental issue today.

◆ Skills Objective

- Inferring

◆ Using the QX3 Microscope you Will...

Capture images of different seed types.

◆ Suggested Materials

QX3 microscope
two labeled cups containing different seed mixtures
paper plate

◆ Safety Tip

Review the safety guidelines in the front of your lab book.

◆ Procedure

1. You will be given two cups of seeds and a paper plate. The seeds in Cup A represent the trees in a section of tropical rain forest. The seeds in Cup B represent the trees in a section of deciduous forest.
2. Pour the seeds from Cup A onto the plate. Sort the seeds by type. Take a snapshot of each type of seed using the QX3 microscope in hand-held mode. Count the different types of seeds. This number represents the number of different kinds of trees in that type of forest.
3. Pour the seeds back into Cup A.
4. Repeat Steps 2 and 3 with the seeds in Cup B.
5. Share your results with your class. Use the class results to calculate the average number of different kinds of seeds in each type of forest.

LIFE SCIENCE

Name ______________________ Date __________ Class ______________

HOW MUCH VARIETY IS THERE? *(continued)*

◆ Data Collection and Observations

Group:	# of Seed Types in Cup A *(Rainforest)*	# of Seed Types in Cup B *(Deciduous Forest)*
1		
2		
3		
4		
5		
6		
Total		
Total / # of Groups = Average		

◆ Analyze and Conclude

1. How does the variety of trees in the "tropical rain forest" compare with the variety of trees in the "deciduous forest"?

____

____

2. Can you suggest any advantages of having a wide variety of species?

____

____

◆ Going Further

Create a poster contrasting the seed diversity from a rainforest with that from a deciduous forest.

LIFE SCIENCE

Name ____________ Date ________ Class ____________

Speeding Up Evaporation

◆ Background

Evaporation is the process by which water vapor enters Earth's atmosphere from the ocean and other surface waters. Rates of evaporation determine the amount of moisture in the atmosphere. Atmospheric moisture in turn affects the formation of clouds and helps to determine whether it will rain.

◆ Skills Objectives

You will be able to:

- develop hypotheses about factors affecting the evaporation of water;
- control variables to determine the effect of different factors;
- draw conclusions about how various factors affect evaporation.

◆ Using the QX3 Microscope you Will...

Make time-lapse movies showing evaporation occurring.

◆ Materials

QX3 microscope
clear plastic metric ruler
plastic petri dish
petri dish cover
plastic dropper
lamp
index card

◆ Safety Tips

Review the safety guidelines in the front of your lab book.

◆ Procedure

Part 1: Effect of Heat

1. How do you think heating a water sample will affect how fast it evaporates? Record your hypothesis in the Data Collection and Observations section as Hypothesis 1.
2. Set the magnification dial on the QX3 microscope to 10X.
3. Place the petri dish on top of the clear plastic ruler on the stage platform, so that the ruler is visible through the dish.
4. Place a drop of water on the petri dish.
5. View the drop of water with the QX3 microscope. Use the ruler to measure the distance across the water drop (diameter) and record this value in the Data Collection and Observations section.

Name ______________________ Date __________ Class __________

SPEEDING UP EVAPORATION *(continued)*

6. Set the time-lapse function on the QX3 microscope to record one image every ten seconds for ten minutes and begin recording.
7. Measure the diameter of the drop of water (if present) at the end of ten minutes and record this in the Data Collection and Observations section.
8. Repeat Steps 1-4 with a lamp placed approximately 15 cm from the petri dish. Try to make this drop of water the same size as the one you started with in Step 3.

Part 2: Effect of Wind

9. How do you think fanning the water will affect how fast it evaporates? Record your hypothesis in the Data Collection & Observations section as 2.
10. Hypothesis Repeat Steps 1-4 while fanning the water drop with an index card. Try to make this drop of water the same size as the other two you have examined.
11. Watch the time-lapse movies to determine the length of time necessary to completely evaporate each of the water drops (if it evaporated completely). Record this in the Data Collection and Observations section.

◆ Data Collection and Observations

Record your observations in the space below.

Hypothesis 1:

____

____

Hypothesis 2:

____

____

Measurement	Droplet without heat or fanning	Droplet with heat	Droplet with fanning
Initial Diameter (mm)			
Final Diameter (mm)			
Time to evaporate (or ten minutes, if not fully evaporated)			

EARTH SCIENCE

Name ______________________ Date ____________ Class ______________

SPEEDING UP EVAPORATION *(continued)*

◆ Analyze and Conclude

1. Did the evidence support both hypotheses? If not, which hypothesis was not supported?

____

____

2. Make a general statement about factors that increase the rate at which water evaporates.

____

____

3. What everyday experiences helped you make your hypotheses at the beginning of the experiment? Explain how hypotheses differ from guesses.

____

____

◆ Going Further

Design an experiment to test other conditions that might affect evaporation rate. Conduct your experiment while making a time-lapse movie with the QX3 microscope.

Name ____________________ Date __________ Class ____________

E2 **SHARPEN YOUR SKILLS**

Classifying

◆ Background

Because there are so many different kinds of minerals, telling them apart can be a challenge. The color of a mineral alone often provides too little information to make an identification. Each mineral has its own specific properties that can be used to identify it. When you have learned to recognize the properties of minerals, you will be able to identify many common minerals. You can see some of the properties of a mineral just by looking at a sample. To observe other properties, however, you need to conduct tests on that sample.

◆ Skills Objectives

- Classifying

◆ Using the QX3 Microscope you Will

Capture images that illustrate color, crystal size, and luster in the minerals examined.

EARTH SCIENCE

◆ Materials

QX3 microscope
penny
talc
calcite
quartz

◆ Safety Tips  *Review the safety guidelines in the front of your lab book.*

◆ Procedure

1. Use your fingernail to try to scratch talc, calcite, and quartz. In the Data Collection and Observations section, record which minerals you were able to scratch.
2. Now try to scratch the minerals with a penny. Were your results different? Explain.
3. Examine the talc, calcite, and quartz samples with the QX3 microscope. Take a snapshot of each sample.

Name ______________________ Date __________ Class __________

CLASSIFYING *(continued)*

◆ Data Collection and Observations

Mineral	Scratched with fingernail (Y or N)	Scratched with penny (Y or N)	Observations
Talc			
Calcite			
Quartz			

◆ Analyze and Conclude

1. Were there any minerals you were unable to scratch with either your fingernail or the penny?

2. How would you classify the three minerals in order of increasing hardness?

◆ Going Further

Create a poster of the various minerals examined with labels describing their properties.

Name ______________________ Date __________ Class ______________

E3 TRY THIS

Crystal Hands

◆ Background

The crystals of each mineral grow atom by atom to form that mineral's particular crystal structure. Geologists classify these structures into six groups, based on the number and angle of the crystal faces. These groups are called crystal systems. For example, all halite crystals are cubic. Halite crystals have six sides that meet at right angles, forming a perfect cube. Sometimes you can see that a crystal has the particular crystal structure of its mineral. Crystals that grow in an open space can be almost perfectly formed.

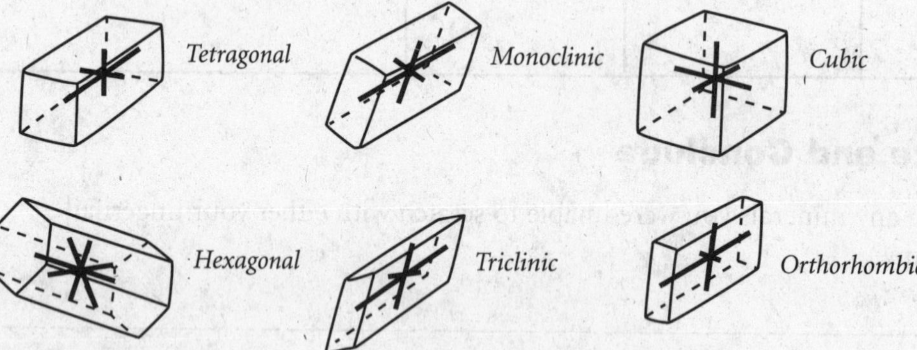

Crystal System

EARTH SCIENCE

◆ Skills Objective

- Observing

◆ Using the QX3 Microscope you Will...

Make a time-lapse movie of the growing of two different salt crystals—Epsom salts and halite.

◆ Materials

QX3 microscope
table salt
Epsom salts
water
2 pitchers
2 shallow pans
piece of black construction paper

Name ______________________ Date __________ Class ______________

CRYSTAL HANDS *(continued)*

◆ Safety Tips    

Review the safety guidelines in the front of your lab book.

◆ Procedure

1. Put on your goggles.
2. Pour a solution of halite (table salt) into one shallow pan and a solution of Epsom salts into another shallow pan.
3. Put a large piece of black construction paper on a flat surface.
4. Dip one hand in the halite solution. Shake off the excess liquid and make a palm print on the paper. Repeat with your other hand and the Epsom salt solution, placing your new print next to the first one. **CAUTION:** *Do not do this activity if you have a cut on your hand. Wash your hands after making your hand prints.*
5. Set up the QX3 microscope so that it can record the crystal formation that occurs as the prints dry. Set the time-lapse interval function for one hour. Let the prints dry overnight.
6. Use the QX3 microscope to compare the shape of the crystals. Take snapshots, and record your observations in the Data Collection and Observations section.

◆ Data Collection and Observations

Solution	Crystal System	Observations
Halite		
Epsom salts		

◆ Analyze and Conclude

1. Which hand print has more crystals?

____

◆ Going Further

Make a poster of the different crystal types observed. Label them with the appropriate crystal system name, as well as their identity.

EARTH SCIENCE

Name ______________________ Date __________ Class ______________

E4 **DISCOVER**

How Does the Rate of Cooling Affect Crystal Growth?

◆ Background

Crystallization is the process by which atoms are arranged to form a material with a crystal structure. Minerals form as hot magma cools inside the Earth's crust, or as lava hardens on the Earth's surface. When magma remains deep below the surface, it cools slowly over many thousands of years. Slow cooling leads to the formation of large crystals. If the crystals remain undisturbed while cooling, they grow by adding atoms according to a regular pattern. Magma closer to the surface cools much faster than magma that hardens deep below ground. With more rapid cooling, there is no time for magma to form large crystals. Instead, small crystals form. If magma erupts to the surface and becomes lava, the lava will also cool quickly and form minerals with small crystals.

◆ Skills Objective

- Relating cause and effect

EARTH SCIENCE

◆ Using the QX3 Microscope you Will...

Make a movie of how cooling affects crystal growth of salol.

◆ Materials

QX3 microscope
salol
plastic spoon
2 microscope slides
tongs
candle
matches
ice cube

◆ Safety Tips

Review the safety guidelines in the front of your lab book.

Name ______________________ Date __________ Class __________

HOW DOES THE RATE OF COOLING... *(continued)*

◆ Procedure

1. Put on your goggles. Use a plastic spoon to place a small amount of salol near one end of each of two microscope slides. You need just enough to form a spot 0.5 to 1.0 cm in diameter.
2. Carefully hold one slide with the tongs. Warm it slowly over a lit candle until the salol is almost completely melted. **CAUTION:** *Move the slide in and out of the flame to avoid cracking the glass.*
3. Set the slide aside to cool slowly.
4. While the first slide is cooling, hold the second slide with tongs and heat it as in Step 2. Cool the slide quickly by placing it on an ice cube. Carefully blow out the candle.
5. Observe the slides with the QX3 microscope. Take snapshots of the crystals on each slide. Compare the appearance of the crystals that form on the two slides, and record your findings in the Data Collection and Observations section.
6. Wash your hands when you are finished.

◆ Data Collection and Observations

Rate of Cooling	Observations
Slow cooling	
Rapid cooling	

◆ Analyze and Conclude

1. Which sample had larger crystals?

____

2. If a mineral forms by rapid cooling, would you expect the crystals to be large or small?

____

◆ Going Further

Make a poster showing the salol crystals formed at different rates. Label the snapshots with the cooling conditions.

EARTH SCIENCE

Name ______________________ Date __________ Class ______________

E5 **DISCOVER**

How Are Rocks Alike or Different?

◆ Background

The Earth's crust is made of rock. Rocks are made of mixtures of minerals and other materials, although some rocks may contain only a single mineral. Granite is made up of the minerals quartz, felspar, mica, and hornblende, and sometimes other minerals. When studying a rock sample, geologists observe the rock's color and texture and determine its mineral composition. Using these characteristics, geologists can classify a rock according to its origin, or where and how it formed.

◆ Skills Objective

- Observing

◆ Using the QX3 Microscope you Will...

Take snapshots of the microscopic structure of marble and conglomerate.

◆ Materials

QX3 microscope
samples of marble and conglomerate
penny

EARTH SCIENCE

◆ Safety Tip

Review the safety guidelines in the front of your lab book.

◆ Procedure

1. Look at samples of marble and conglomerate using the QX3 microscope. Take a snapshot of each.
2. Describe the two rocks. What is the color and texture of each?
3. Try scratching the surface of each rock with the edge of a penny. Which rock seems harder?
4. Hold each rock in your hand. Allowing for the fact that the samples aren't exactly the same size, which rock seems denser?

Name ______________________ Date __________ Class ______________

HOW ARE ROCKS ALIKE OR DIFFERENT? *(continued)*

◆ Data Collection and Observations

Rock	Color/Texture	Hardness	Density	Notes
Marble				
Conglomerate				

◆ Analyze and Conclude

1. Based on your observations, how would you compare the physical properties of marble and conglomerate?

____

____

◆ Going Further

Create a poster that illustrates the composition of marble and conglomerate.

EARTH SCIENCE

Name ______________________ Date __________ Class __________

E6 **DISCOVER**

How do Igneous Rocks Form?

◆ Background

The first rocks to form on Earth probably looked much like the igneous rocks that harden from lava today. Igneous rock is any rock that forms from magma or lava. The name "igneous" comes from the Latin word ignis, meaning "fire." Most igneous rocks are made of mineral crystals. The only exceptions to this rule are the different types of volcanic glass—igneous rock that lacks minerals with a crystal structure. Igneous rocks are classified according to their origin, texture, and mineral composition.

◆ Skills Objectives

- Inferring

◆ Using the QX3 Microscope you Will...

Capture images of rock types and make predictions about their formation, based on their microscopic appearance.

EARTH SCIENCE

◆ Materials

QX3 microscope
granite
obsidian

◆ Safety Tips

Review the safety guidelines in the front of your lab book.

◆ Procedure

1. Use the QX3 microscope to examine samples of granite and obsidian.
2. In the Data Collection and Observations section, describe the texture of both rocks using the terms coarse, fine, or glassy.
3. Which rock has coarse-grained crystals? Which rock has no crystals or grains?

HOW DO IGNEOUS ROCKS FORM? *(continued)*

◆ Data Collection and Observations

Sample	Description	Observations
Granite		
Obsidian		

◆ Analyze and Conclude

1. Granite and obsidian are igneous rocks. Given the physical properties of these rocks, what can you infer about how each type of rock formed?

____

____

____

◆ Going Further

Create a poster of the various rock types and label them with their methods of formation.

EARTH SCIENCE

Name ______________________ Date __________ Class ______________

E7 **TRY THIS**

Rock Absorber

◆ Background

Most sedimentary rocks are made up of the broken pieces of other rocks. A clastic rock is a sedimentary rock that forms when rock fragments are squeezed together. These fragments can range in size from clay particles too small to be seen without a microscope to large boulders too heavy for you to lift. Clastic rocks are grouped by the size of the rock fragments, or particles of which they are made.

◆ Skills Objective

- Drawing conclusions

◆ Using the QX3 Microscope you Will...

Capture images of the microscopic structure of sandstone and shale.

◆ Materials

EARTH SCIENCE

QX3 microscope
sandstone
shale
balance
pan
water

◆ Safety Tip

Review the safety guidelines in the front of your lab book.

◆ Procedure

1. Using the QX3 microscope, observe samples of sandstone and shale. How are they alike? How are they different? Take snapshots of each.
2. Use a balance to measure the mass of each rock.
3. Place the rocks in a pan of water. Observe the samples. Which sample has bubbles escaping? Predict which sample will gain mass.
4. Leave the rocks submerged in the pan overnight.
5. The next day, remove the rocks from the pan and find the mass of each rock.

Name ______________________ Date __________ Class ______________

ROCK ABSORBER *(continued)*

◆ Data Collection and Observations

Rock	Initial Mass	New Mass	Observations
Sandstone			
Shale			

◆ Analyze and Conclude

1. How did the masses of the two rocks change after soaking?

____

____

2. What can you conclude about each rock based on your observations?

____

____

◆ Going Further

Create a poster that illustrates the microscopic differences between fine-grained and coarse-grained rocks.

Name ______________________ Date __________ Class ______________

E8 DISCOVER

How Do the Grain Patterns of Gneiss and Granite Compare?

◆ Background

Heat and pressure deep beneath the Earth's surface can change any rock into metamorphic rock. When rock changes into metamorphic rock, its appearance, texture, crystal structure, and mineral content change. Metamorphic rock can form out of igneous, sedimentary, or other metamorphic rock. While metamorphic rocks are forming, high temperatures change the size and shape of the grains, or mineral crystals, in the rock. In addition, tremendous pressure squeezes rock so tightly that the mineral grains may line up in flat, parallel layers. Geologists classify metamorphic rocks by the arrangement of the grains that make up the rocks.

Granite

Gneiss

EARTH SCIENCE

◆ Skills Objective

- Inferring

◆ Using the QX3 Microscope you Will...

Capture images of the grain structure of gneiss and granite.

◆ Materials

QX3 microscope
gneiss samples
granite samples

◆ Safety Tip  *Review the safety guidelines in the front of your lab book.*

◆ Procedure

1. Using the QX3 microscope, observe samples of gneiss and granite. Take snapshots of each. Look carefully at the grains or crystals in both rocks.
2. Observe how the grains or crystals are arranged in both rocks. Draw a sketch of both rocks and describe their textures.

Name ______________ Date ________ Class ____________

HOW DO THE GRAIN PATTERNS... *(continued)*

◆ Data Collection and Observations

Rock	Description	Sketch
Gneiss		
Granite		

◆ Analyze and Conclude

1. Within the crust, some granite becomes gneiss. What do you think must happen to cause this change?

____

____

◆ Going Further

Create a poster that illustrates the relationship between gneiss and granite. Label the illustrations appropriately.

Name ______________________ Date __________ Class ______________

E9 **DISCOVER**

What Can You Conclude From the Way a Rock Reacts to Acid?

◆ Background

The hard shells of living things produce some kinds of limestone. How does limestone form? In the ocean, many living things, including coral, clams, oysters, and snails, have shells or skeletons made of calcite. When these animals die, their shells pile up as sediment on the ocean floor. Over millions of years, these layers of sediment can grow to a depth of hundreds of meters. Slowly, the pressure of overlying layers compacts the sediment. Some of the shells dissolve, forming a solution of calcite that seeps into the spaces between the shell fragments. Later, the dissolved material comes out of solution, forming calcite. The calcite cements the shell particles together, forming limestone.

◆ Skills Objectives

- Drawing conclusions

EARTH SCIENCE

◆ Using the QX3 Microscope you Will...

Capture images of the microscopic structure of limestone and coquina.

◆ Materials

QX3 microscope
samples of limestone and coquina
dilute (5%) hydrochloric acid
plastic dropper
running water

◆ Safety Tips

Review the safety guidelines in the front of your lab book.

◆ Procedure

1. Using the QX3 microscope, observe the color and texture of samples of limestone and coquina. Take snapshots of each.
2. Put on your goggles and apron.
3. Obtain a small amount of dilute hydrochloric acid from your teacher. Hydrochloric acid is used to test rocks for the presence of the mineral calcite.
4. Using a plastic dropper, place a few drops of dilute hydrochloric acid on the limestone. **CAUTION:** *Hydrochloric acid can cause burns.*

Name ______________________ Date __________ Class ______________

WHAT CAN YOU CONCLUDE FROM THE WAY... *(continued)*

5. Record your observations in the Data Collection and Observations section.
6. Repeat Steps 2 through 4 with the sample of coquina, and observe the results.
7. Rinse the samples of limestone and coquina with lots of water before returning them to your teacher. Wash your hands.

◆ Data Collection and Observations

Record your observations in the space below.

Observations of interaction of hydrochloric acid and limestone:

Observations of interaction of hydrochloric acid and coquina:

◆ Analyze and Conclude

1. How did the color and texture of the two rocks compare?

____

____

2. How did the rocks react to the test?

____

____

3. A piece of coral reacts to hydrochloric acid the same way as limestone and coquina. What could you conclude about the mineral composition of coral?

____

____

◆ Going Further

Assemble a slideshow of snapshots of calcite containing rocks, based on further experimentation.

EARTH SCIENCE

Name ______________________ Date __________ Class ______________

E10 DISCOVER

What are Volcanic Rocks Like?

◆ Background

Lava begins as magma in the Earth's mantle. There, magma forms in the asthenosphere, which lies beneath the lithosphere. The materials of the asthenosphere are under great pressure. As magma rises toward the surface, the pressure decreases. The dissolved gases begin to separate out, forming bubbles. A volcano erupts when an opening develops in weak rock on the surface. During a volcanic eruption, the gases dissolved in magma rush out, carrying the magma with them. Once magma reaches the surface and becomes lava, the gases bubble out.

◆ Skills Objectives

- Developing hypotheses

◆ Using the QX3 Microscope you Will...

Capture images of volcanic rocks.

EARTH SCIENCE

◆ Materials

QX3 microscope
samples of pumice and obsidian

◆ Safety Tips  *Review the safety guidelines in the front of your lab book.*

◆ Procedure

1. Observe samples of pumice and obsidian with the QX3 microscope. Take a snapshot of each, and note your observations in the Data Collection and Observations section.
2. How would you describe the texture of the pumice? What could have caused this texture?
3. Observe the surface of the obsidian. How does the surface of the obsidian differ from pumice?

Name ______________________ Date __________ Class __________

WHAT ARE VOLCANIC ROCKS LIKE? *(continued)*

◆ Data Collection and Observations

	Texture/Surface Appearance	Observations/Notes
Pumice		
Obsidian		

◆ Analyze and Conclude

1. What could have produced the difference in texture between the two rocks? Explain your answer.

____

____

____

◆ Going Further

Create a poster that shows the features of volcanic rock compared to other types of rock.

EARTH SCIENCE

Name ______________________ Date __________ Class ______________

E11 TRY THIS

Rusting Away

◆ Background

Chemical weathering is the process that breaks down rock through chemical changes. The agents of chemical weathering include water, oxygen, carbon dioxide, living organisms, and acid rain. Chemical weathering produces rock particles that have a different mineral makeup from the rock they came from. Each rock is made up of one or more minerals. For example, granite is made up of several minerals, including feldspar, quartz, and mica. But chemical weathering of granite eventually changes the feldspar minerals to clay minerals.

◆ Skills Objective

- Predicting

◆ Using the QX3 Microscope you Will...

Make a time-lapse movie of rust occurring on steel wool.

◆ Materials

QX3 microscope
2 pads of steel wool
water
plastic wrap
plastic plate

EARTH SCIENCE

◆ Safety Tip

Review the safety guidelines in the front of your lab book.

◆ Procedure

1. Moisten some steel wool and cover it loosely with plastic wrap so that it will not dry out.
2. Place the wrapped steel wool onto the plastic plate. Place the plate on the stage platform of the QX3 microscope. Record your observations in the Data and Observations section. Begin a time-lapse movie with the QX3 microscope set at 10X magnification and recording intervals of 1 hour.
3. Observe the steel wool after two or three days, and record your observations in the Data and Observations section. What has happened to the steel wool?
4. Take a new piece of steel wool and squeeze it between your fingers. Record your observations in the Data and Observations section. Remove the steel wool from the plastic wrap and squeeze it between your fingers. What happens? Record your observations. Wash your hands when you have finished.

Name ______________________ Date __________ Class ______________

RUSTING AWAY *(continued)*

◆ Data Collection and Observations

Steel wool	Observations
Initial appearance of steel wool	
Appearance of steel wool after soaking	
Observations when new steel wool is squeezed	
Observations when soaked steel wool is squeezed	

◆ Analyze and Conclude

1. If you kept the steel wool moist for a longer period of time, what would eventually happen to it?

____

____

2. How is the weathering of steel wool like the weathering of rocks?

____

____

◆ Going Further

Record subsequent time-lapse movies that show what eventually happens to the soaked steel wool pad.

Name ______________________ Date __________ Class ______________

E12 DISCOVER

What is Soil?

◆ Background

A crack in a rock seems to have little in common with a flower garden containing thick, rich soil. But soil is what the weathered rock and other materials in the crack have started to become. Soil is the loose, weathered material on the Earth's surface, in which plants can grow. Soil forms as rock is broken down by weathering and mixes with other materials on the surface. Soil is constantly being formed wherever bedrock is exposed. Bedrock is the solid layer of rock beneath the soil. Once exposed at the surface, bedrock gradually weathers into smaller and smaller particles that are the basic material of soil.

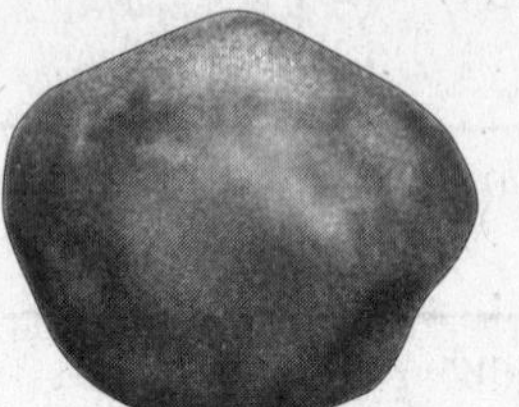

◆ Skills Objective

- Forming operational definitions

◆ Using the QX3 Microscope you Will...

Capture images of soil.

EARTH SCIENCE

◆ Materials

QX3 microscope
soil sample
paper cup
paper plate or towel
toothpick

◆ Safety Tips

  *Review the safety guidelines in the front of your lab book.*

◆ Procedure

1. Use a toothpick to separate a sample of soil into individual particles. Examine them with the QX3 microscope. Try to identify the different types of particles in the sample and record them in the Data Collection and Observations section. Take snapshots of the different types of particles you see. Wash your hands when you are finished.

Name ______________________ Date __________ Class ______________

WHAT IS SOIL? *(continued)*

2. In the Data Collection and Observations section, write a "recipe" for the sample of soil, naming each of the "ingredients" that you think the soil contains. Include what percentage of each ingredient would be needed to re-create the soil.
3. Compare your recipe with those of your classmates.

◆ Data Collection and Observations

Record your observations in the space below.

Particle types observed in the soil sample:

____

____

"Recipe" for soil:

____

____

◆ Analyze and Conclude

1. Based on your observations, how would you define soil?

____

____

◆ Going Further

Make a poster labeled with soil particle types and their "recipe" proportions.

Name ____________________ Date __________ Class __________

E13 REAL WORLD LAB

Getting to Know the Soil

◆ Background

Soil is more than just particles of weathered bedrock. Soil is a mixture of rock particles, minerals, decayed organic material, air, and water. The type of rock particles and minerals in any given soil depends on two factors: the bedrock that was weathered to form the soil and the type of weathering. Together, sand, silt, and clay make up the portion of soil that comes from weathered rock. The decayed organic material in soil is humus. Humus is a dark-colored substance that forms as plant and animal remains decay. Humus helps create spaces in soil for the air and water that plants must have. Humus is also rich in the nitrogen, sulfur, phosphorus, and potassium that plants need to grow.

◆ Skills Objectives

- Observing
- Inferring
- Posing questions

EARTH SCIENCE

◆ Using the QX3 Microscope you Will...

Capture images that illustrate the various components of soil.

◆ Materials

QX3 microscope
20-30 grams of soil
plastic spoon
plastic dropper
toothpick
water
graph paper rules with 1 or 2 mm spacing
plastic petri dish or jar lid

◆ Safety Tips

Review the safety guidelines in the front of your lab book.

Name ______________________ Date __________ Class ______________

GETTING TO KNOW THE SOIL *(continued)*

◆ Procedure

1. Your teacher will give you a dry sample of soil. As you observe the sample, record your observations in the Data and Observations section.
2. Spread half of the sample on the graph paper. Spread the soil thinly so that you can see the lines on the paper through the soil. Using graph paper as a background, estimate the sizes of the particles that make up the soil. Use the QX3 microscope in hand-held mode to collect snapshots of these particles sizes.
3. Place the rest of the sample in the palm of your hand, rub it between your fingers, and squeeze. Is it soft or gritty? Does it clump together or crumble when you squeeze it?
4. Place about half the sample in a plastic petri dish on the stage platform of the QX3 microscope. Using the dropper, add water one drop at a time. Take a snapshot after each addition of water. Watch how the sample changes. Does any material in the sample float? As the sample gets wet, do you notice any odor?
5. Look at some of the dry soil under the QX3 microscope. Use the toothpick to examine the particles in the soil. Take a snapshot, and label it with the particles, such as gravel, organic matter, or strangely shaped grains.
6. Clean up and dispose of your soil sample as directed by your teacher. **CAUTION:** *Wash your hands when you finish handling the soil.*

EARTH SCIENCE

◆ Data Collection and Observations

Sample Characteristics	Observations/ Notes
Range of particle sizes	
Texture of dry sample	
Texture of wet sample	
Particle types present in sample	
Odor	
Other	

Name ______________________ Date __________ Class ______________

GETTING TO KNOW THE SOIL *(continued)*

◆ Analyze and Conclude

1. What did you notice about the appearance of the soil sample when you first obtained it?

____

____

2. What can you infer about the composition of the soil from the different sizes of its particles? From your observations of its texture? From how the sample changed when water was added? What surprised you the most about the composition of your sample?

____

____

____

____

3. Based on the composition of your soil sample, can you determine the type of environment from which it was taken?

____

____

4. List several questions that a soil scientist would need to answer to determine whether a soil sample was good for growing flowers or vegetables. Did your observations answer these questions for your soil sample?

____

____

◆ Going Further

Repeat the procedure using a soil sample from a different location. Organize your findings into a slide show or poster of soil characteristics including both samples. How does the new soil compare with the first soil sample you tested?

EARTH SCIENCE

Name ______________________ Date __________ Class __________

E14 **DISCOVER**

What Can Be Learned from Beach Sand?

◆ Background

Waves not only erode the land, they also deposit sediment. Waves shape the coast through both erosion and deposition. Deposition occurs when waves slow down and the water drops its sediment. This process is similar to the deposition that occurs on a river delta when the river slows down and drops its sediment load. As waves reach the shore, they drop the sediment they carry, forming a beach. A beach is an area of wave-washed sediment along a coast. The sediment deposited on beaches is usually sand. Most sand comes from rivers that carry eroded particles of rock into the ocean.

◆ Skills Objective

- Posing questions

◆ Using the QX3 Microscope you Will...

Capture images of beach sand showing the different components of the sand.

◆ Materials

QX3 microscope
sand from two beaches
plastic spoon
petri dish

◆ Safety Tip  *Review the safety guidelines in the front of your lab book.*

◆ Procedure

1. Collect a spoonful of sand from one of the two beach sand samples that your teacher has provided.
2. Examine the first sample of beach sand with the QX3 microscope.
3. Record the properties of the sand grains, for example, color and shape in the Data and Observations section. Are the grains smooth and rounded or angular and rough? Are all the grains in the sample the same shape and color?
4. Return the first sample to the container you collected it from. Collect a spoonful of sand from the other beach sand sample, and repeat Steps 2-3. How do the two samples compare?

EARTH SCIENCE

Name ______________________ Date __________ Class ______________

WHAT CAN BE LEARNED FROM BEACH SAND? *(continued)*

◆ Data Collection and Observations

Sample	Particle Color	Particle Shape	Notes
Beach 1			
Beach 2			

◆ Analyze and Conclude

1. What questions do you need to answer to understand beach sand? Use what you know about erosion and deposition to help you think of questions.

____

____

EARTH SCIENCE

◆ Going Further

Make a poster showing the components found in beach sand. Label each component.

Name ______________________ Date __________ Class ______________

E15 DISCOVER

What's in a Rock?

◆ Background

Fossils are the preserved remains, or traces, of living things. Fossils provide evidence of how life has changed over time. Fossils also help scientists infer how the Earth's surface has changed. Fossils are clues to what past environments were like. Most fossils form when living things die and are buried by sediments. The sediments slowly harden into rock and preserve the shapes of the organisms. Scientists who study fossils are called paleontologists. Fossils are usually found in sedimentary rock.

◆ Skills Objectives

- Inferring

◆ Using the QX3 Microscope you Will...

Capture images of the microscopic components of rocks.

◆ Materials

QX3 microscope
rock sample containing fossils

◆ Safety Tips  *Review the safety guidelines in the front of your lab book.*

◆ Procedure

1. Use the QX3 microscope to carefully observe the rock sample provided by your teacher. Take a snapshot of the rock's interesting features.
2. In the Data Collection and Observations section, make a drawing of any shapes you see in the rock. Include as many details as you can. Beneath your drawing, write a short description of what you see.

EARTH SCIENCE

Name ______________________ Date __________ Class ______________

WHAT'S IN A ROCK? *(continued)*

◆ Data Collection and Observations

Record your observations in the space below.

Description:

____

____

____

EARTH SCIENCE

◆ Analyze and Conclude

1. What do you think the rock contains?

____

____

2. How do you think the shapes you observed in the rock got there?

____

____

◆ Going Further

Create a poster of fossil remains in rocks.

Name ______________________ Date __________ Class ______________

E16 **DISCOVER**

What's in a Piece of Coal?

◆ Background

Coal is a solid fossil fuel formed from plant remains. People have burned coal to produce heat for thousands of years. However, coal was only a minor source of energy compared to wood until the 1800s. As Europe and the United States entered the Industrial Revolution, the need for fuel increased rapidly. As forests were cut down, firewood became more expensive. It became worthwhile to find, mine, and transport coal. Coal fueled the huge steam engines that powered trains, ships, and factories during the Industrial Revolution. Today, coal provides 23 percent of the energy used in the United States. The major use of coal is to fuel electric power plants.

◆ Skills Objectives

- Observing

◆ Using the QX3 Microscope you Will...

Capture microscopic images of the structure and composition of coal.

◆ Materials

QX3 microscope
lignite coal

◆ Safety Tips

Review the safety guidelines in the front of your lab book.

◆ Procedure

1. Observe a chunk of coal. Record your observations in the Data Collection and Observations section in as much detail as possible, including color, texture, and shape.
2. Now use the QX3 microscope to observe the coal more closely. Take a snapshot of interesting features in the coal.
3. Examine your coal for fossils, and imprints of plant or animal remains.

EARTH SCIENCE

Name ______________________ Date __________ Class ______________

WHAT'S IN A PIECE OF COAL? *(continued)*

◆ Data Collection and Observations

Coal Type:	Color	Texture	Observations
Lignite			

◆ Analyze and Conclude

What did you notice when you used the QX3 microscope compared to your first observations? What do you think coal is made of?

◆ Going Further

Devise a model showing how fossil fuels form over time. Find out what happens to buried materials to turn them into fossil fuels.

EARTH SCIENCE

Name ____________________ Date __________ Class ____________

E17 DISCOVER

What's in Pond Water?

◆ Background

Water is a large part of every living thing. Water makes up nearly 2/3 of your body. That water is necessary to keep your body functioning. Water is essential for living things to grow, reproduce, and carry out other important processes. Many living things use water as a home. An organism's habitat is the place where it lives. A habitat provides the things an organism needs to survive. Both fresh water and salt water provide habitats for many different types of living things.

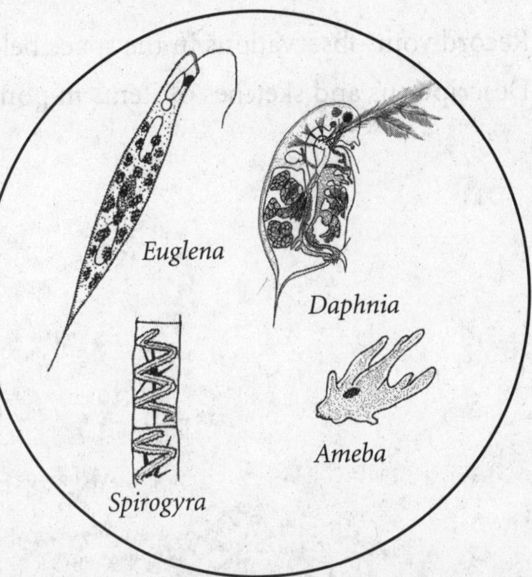

Common Pond Organisms

◆ Skills Objective

You will be able to:

- use a system to classify organisms found in pond water.

◆ Using the QX3 Microscope you Will...

Capture images of microlife forms found in pond water.

◆ Materials

QX3 microscope
pond water
plastic petri dish
eyedropper
slide
coverslip

◆ Safety Tips

   *Review the safety guidelines in the front of your lab book.*

◆ Procedure

1. Using the QX3 microscope, observe a sample of pond water in a petri dish at 10X magnification.
2. Make a list of everything you see in the water. If you don't know the name of something, write a short description or draw a picture. Take snapshots.
3. Place one or two drops of pond water on a microscope slide, and add a coverslip.
4. Observe the slide with the QX3 microscope at 60X magnification. Record your observations, or make sketches. Take snapshots of interesting items.

EARTH SCIENCE

Name ______________________ Date __________ Class __________

WHAT'S IN POND WATER? *(continued)*

◆ Data Collection and Observations

Record your observations in the space below.

Descriptions and sketches of items in pond water (include magnification):

◆ Analyze and Conclude

1. Use one of these systems to divide the items on your list into two groups: moving/still, living/nonliving, or microscopic/visible without a microscope.

____

____

2. What does your classification system tell you about pond water?

____

____

◆ Going Further

Collect water from different outdoor habitats. Examine the samples for life forms. Make a poster showing the diversity of microlife in local habitats.

EARTH SCIENCE

Name ______________________ Date __________ Class ______________

E18 **TRY THIS**

Modeling a Humid Climate

◆ Background

The warmest temperate marine climates are on the edges of the tropics. Humid subtropical climates are wet and warm, but not as constantly hot as the tropics. The southeastern United States has a humid subtropical climate. Summers are hot, with much more rainfall than in winter. Maritime tropical air masses move inland, bringing tropical weather conditions, including thunderstorms and occasional hurricanes, to southern cities, such as Houston, New Orleans, and Atlanta.

◆ Skills Objective

- Inferring

◆ Using the QX3 Microscope you Will...

Make a time-lapse movie of humidity occurring within a covered bowl.

◆ Materials

QX3 microscope
2 small plastic bowls
clear plastic wrap
2 rubber bands

◆ Safety Tip  *Review the safety guidelines in the front of your lab book.*

◆ Procedure

1. Put the same amount of water in each of two small plastic bowls.
2. Place a sheet of transparent plastic wrap over each bowl. Secure each sheet with a rubber band.
3. Place one bowl on a warm, sunny windowsill or near a radiator. Prop the QX3 microscope so that the clear plastic wrap over the bowl is in the field of view. Set the time-lapse record function to record at one-hour intervals. Put the other bowl in a cool location.
4. Wait a day and then look at the two bowls. What do you see on the plastic wrap over each bowl?

EARTH SCIENCE

Name ______________________ Date __________ Class ______________

◆ Data Collection and Observations

Bowl after 1 day	Observations
Cool location	
Warm location	

◆ Analyze and Conclude

1. Would you expect to find more water vapor in the air in a warm climate or in a cool one? Why? Explain your results in terms of solar energy.

____

____

EARTH SCIENCE

◆ Going Further

Keep the bowls in the same places, but remove the plastic wrap. Set the QX3 microscope to record the water level in the bowl in the warm spot at one-hour intervals. Check on the bowls after one or two days. What has happened to the water level?

Name ______________________ Date __________ Class ______________

E19 **DISCOVER**

What Story Can Tree Rings Tell?

◆ Background

Tree rings can be used to learn about ancient climates. Every summer, a tree grows a new layer of wood under its bark. These layers form rings when seen in a cross section, as shown below. In cool climates, the amount the tree grows—the thickness of a ring—depends on the length of the warm growing season. In dry climates, the thickness of each ring depends on the amount of rainfall. By looking at cross sections of trees, scientists can count backward from the outer ring to see whether previous years were warm or cool, wet or dry. A thin ring indicates that the year was cool or dry. A thick ring indicates that a year was warm or wet.

Tree rings

◆ Skills Objective

- Inferring

◆ Using the QX3 Microscope you Will...

Capture microscopic images of tree rings.

◆ Materials

QX3 microscope

◆ Safety Tip

Review the safety guidelines in the front of your lab book.

◆ Procedure

1. Look at the photo of tree rings in your textbook. Tree rings are the layers of new wood that form each year as a tree grows.
2. Use the QX3 microscope to closely study the tree rings. Note whether they are all the same thickness.
3. What weather conditions might cause a tree to form thicker or thinner tree rings?

EARTH SCIENCE

WHAT STORY CAN TREE RINGS TELL? *(continued)*

◆ Data Collection and Observations

	Observations
Tree rings	

◆ Analyze and Conclude

1. How could you use tree rings to tell you about weather in the past?

____

____

◆ Going Further

EARTH SCIENCE

Examine real tree trunk sections. Take snapshots of different stem or trunk sections and examine the tree rings. Make a poster showing tree rings from one of the trunks. You can also construct a "climate time line" using the information in the tree rings.

Name ______________________ Date __________ Class ______________

P 1 **DISCOVER**

What Properties Help You Sort Matter?

◆ Background

Each specific substance has its own combination of properties that can be used to identify it. For example, you could tell whether or not a particular substance is water by its properties. Water is a clear, colorless liquid at room temperature. At temperatures of 0°C or lower, water changes into ice. At temperatures of 100°C or higher, water changes into water vapor, an invisible gas. Investigating properties like these is one of the jobs that chemists do. Chemistry is the study of the properties of matter and how matter changes.

◆ Skills Objectives

- Classifying

◆ Using the QX3 Microscope you Will...

Examine the microscopic features of different objects to help determine their properties.

◆ Materials

QX3 microscope
wax candles
playing cards
vials of water
inflated balloon
aluminum foil
coins
small rocks
pencils
paper clips

◆ Safety Tips  *Review the safety guidelines in the front of your lab book.*

◆ Procedure

1. Carefully examine the ten objects that your teacher provides. Use the QX3 microscope to examine each object's microscopic appearance. Write a brief description of each object in the Data Collection and Observations section. What properties are unique to each object? What properties do some objects have in common?
2. Which objects appear to be made of a single substance? Which objects appear to be mixtures of different substances?

PHYSICAL SCIENCE

Name ______________________ Date __________ Class __________

WHAT PROPERTIES HELP YOU SORT MATTER? *(continued)*

3. Divide the objects into small groups so that the objects in each group share one of the properties you identified.

◆ Data Collection and Observations

Item	Description	Unique Properties	Shared Properties	Single Substance or Mixture?

◆ Analyze and Conclude

PHYSICAL SCIENCE

1. Share your observations and grouping with your classmates. How do the ways your classmates grouped the objects compare with the way you grouped the objects? Think of at least one other way to group the objects.

____

____

____

◆ Going Further

Create more than one poster showing the different ways of grouping these items. Be sure to include labels that reflect your reasoning for classifying the objects into the groups that you chose.

Name ______________________ Date __________ Class ______________

Observing

◆ Background

One of the first people to observe cells was the English scientist and inventor, Robert Hooke. In 1663, Hooke observed the structure of a thin slice of cork using a compound microscope he had built himself. Cork, the bark of the cork oak tree, is made up of cells that are no longer alive. To Hooke, the cork looked like tiny rectangular rooms, which he called cells.

◆ Skills Objectives

You will be able to:

- observe and draw cells and organisms.

◆ Using the QX3 Microscope you Will...

Capture images of thin slices of cork and various living cells.

◆ Materials

QX3 microscope
prepared slide of cork cells
lettuce
water
pond water
plastic dropper
slide
cover slip

◆ Safety Tips   *Review the safety guidelines in the front of your lab book.*

◆ Procedure

1. Place a prepared slide of a thin slice of cork on the stage of the QX3 microscope.
2. Observe the slide under 60X magnification. Count the number of cells that fit end to end in the field of view. Draw what you see through the microscope in the Data Collection and Observations section. Take a snapshot.
3. Put a small, very thick piece of lettuce on a slide. Repeat Step 2.
4. Place a few drops of pond water on another slide and cover it with a coverslip. Repeat Step 2.
5. Wash your hands after handling pond water.

OBSERVING *(continued)*

◆ Data Collection and Observations

Cork cell drawing

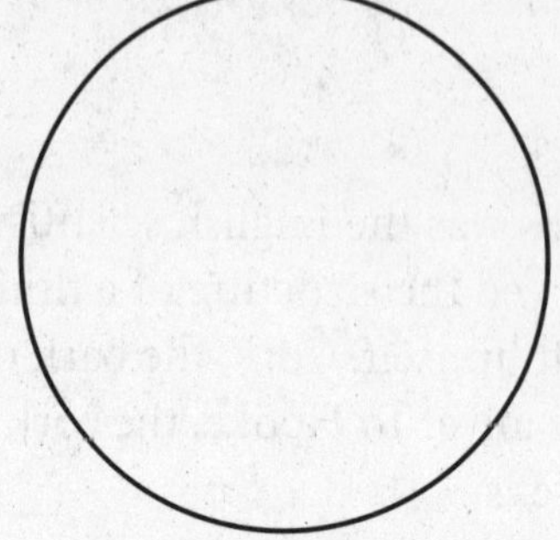

Lettuce cell drawing

Pond water drawing

	Cork	**Lettuce**
# Cells that fit across field of view		

◆ Analyze and Conclude

1. How does your drawing of cork cells compare to Hooke's drawing in your textbook?

____

____

2. Based upon your observations of pond water, why did Leeuwenhoek call the organisms he saw "little animals"?

____

____

PHYSICAL SCIENCE

◆ Going Further

Make a poster of cells using the snapshots you took with the QX3 microscope. Label snapshots with the source of the cells.

Name ______________________ Date __________ Class ______________

P3 **TRY THIS**

Crystal Shapes

◆ Background

In an ionic compound, every ion is attracted to ions near it that have an opposite charge. Positive ions tend to be near negative ions and farther from other positive ions. As a result, a positive sodium ion doesn't bond with just one negative chloride ion. It bonds with ions above, below, and to all sides. Because chloride ions bond with sodium ions in the same way, a crystal forms. This pattern continues, no matter what the size of the crystal. In a single grain of salt, the crystal can extend for millions of ions in every direction.

◆ Skills Objectives

- Observing

◆ Using the QX3 Microscope you Will...

Examine the microscopic structure of various ionic compounds.

◆ Materials

- QX3 microscope
- halite
- fluorite
- sodium iodide
- potassium iodide
- black paper
- plastic spoons

◆ Safety Tips

Review the safety guidelines in the front of your lab book.

PHYSICAL SCIENCE

◆ Procedure

1. Use a spoon to place a small amount of halite (NaCl) crystals on a piece of black paper.
2. Use the QX3 microscope to carefully examine the structure of the crystals. Take a snapshot of the crystals at each magnification.
3. In the Data Collection and Observations section, draw and label a picture of what you see.
4. Repeat Steps 1 through 3 with samples of other crystals provided by your teacher.

CRYSTAL SHAPES *(continued)*

◆ Data Collection and Observations

Record your observations in the space below.

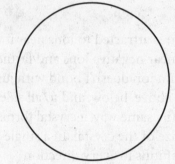

◆ Analyze and Conclude

1. Do the shapes of the crystals vary within a sample?

____

____

2. Do the shapes vary from one sample to another? Explain.

____

____

◆ Going Further

Create a slide show of the crystal snapshots that you collected. Be sure to label each slide with the name of the substance and the magnification of the snapshot.

Name ______________________ Date __________ Class ____________

P 4 SKILLS LAB

Shape Up!

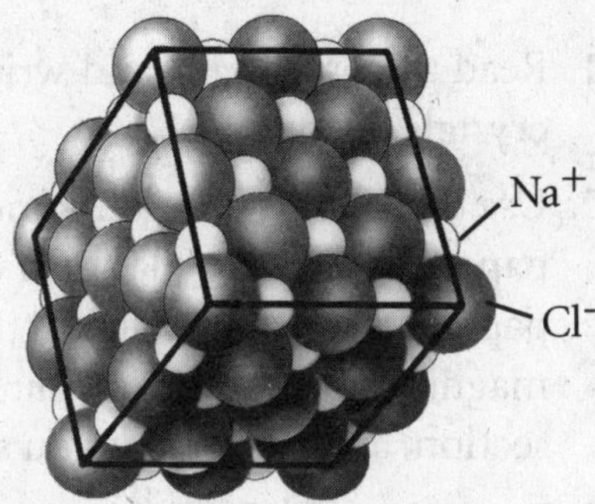

A halite crystal contains sodium and chloride ions in an alternating pattern.

◆ Background

Halite, or table salt, is an ionic compound. All halite samples have sharp edges, corners, and flat surfaces. These properties result from how the ions are arranged. In solid sodium chloride (NaCl), the Na^+ and Cl^- ions come together in an alternating pattern, as shown in the diagram. The ions form an orderly, 3-dimensional arrangement called a crystal.

◆ Skills Objectives

You will be able to:

- make a prediction based on your observations and knowledge;
- interpret observations of crystals;
- draw conclusions regarding the characteristic nature of crystal structure in an ionic compound.

◆ Using the QX3 Microscope you Will...

Make a time-lapse movie of the evaporation of water from a salt solution and capture images of salt crystals before and after the experiment.

◆ Materials

QX3 microscope
sodium chloride
small plastic spoon
two petri dishes
black paper
100 mL graduated cylinder
250mL beaker
labeling marker
water (80°C)

◆ Safety Tips    

Review the safety guidelines in the front of your lab book.

PHYSICAL SCIENCE

Name ______________________ Date __________ Class ______________

◆ Procedure

1. Read the procedure, and write a prediction about the appearance of the crystals in Step 7.
2. Use a spoon to sprinkle some sodium chloride in a petri dish. Place black paper on the stage platform of the QX3 microscope. Put the dish on the black paper. Observe the salt with the QX3 microscope. Take snapshots at different magnifications. Record your observations in the Data and Observations section, and draw what you see.
3. Pour 100 mL of hot water (80°C) into a 250 mL beaker. Add about 1/2 a spoonful of salt to the water and stir until it dissolves. Record your observations of the solution in the Data and Observations section.
4. Add the rest of the salt and stir well. Let any undissolved salt particles settle at the bottom of the beaker.
5. Carefully pour off 50 mL of the solution into a petri dish labeled with your name.
6. Place the petri dish on top of the black paper on the stage of the QX3 microscope set at 10X magnification. Begin recording a time-lapse movie at intervals of 30 minutes. Let the uncovered petri dish sit overnight, or until all the water has evaporated.
7. Record your observations in the Data and Observations section, take a final snapshot, and draw what you see.

◆ Data Collection and Observations

Substance	Observations
Original NaCl crystals	
NaCl solution	
New NaCl crystals	

Name _______________ Date _______ Class _______

SHAPE UP! *(continued)*

◆ Analyze and Conclude

1. Use the chart to examine and evaluate your information. How did the appearance of the sodium chloride change between Steps 2 and 3? Explain that change in terms of the ions that make up the compound.

2. Describe the shapes of the crystals you observed in Step 7, along with any patterns you see within any of the crystals.

3. Compare and contrast the crystals you observed in Step 2 and Step 7.

4. Use what you know about ionic compounds to explain the shapes of the new crystals. Would you expect all sodium chloride crystals to have the same shapes? Explain.

5. Could you use the results of this experiment to draw conclusions about the crystals formed by other ionic compounds? Explain.

◆ Going Further

Does the original temperature of the sodium chloride solution affect crystal formation? Design a safe experiment comparing solutions of ice water, tap water, and hot water. Be sure to take snapshots of the crystals with the QX3 microscope both before and after the experiment. Obtain your teacher's approval before trying this experiment.

Name ______________________ Date __________ Class __________

P 5 DISCOVER

How Small Do They Get?

◆ Background

Every mineral has a crystal structure. The repeating pattern of particles creates a shape that may be visible to your eye, or you may have to look under a microscope to see it. Either way, the structure of the crystal is a characteristic property of the mineral. Mineral crystals may be made up of ions, or they may contain atoms that are covalently bonded together. The arrangement of particles in a mineral and the kind of bonds holding them together determine physical properties, such as crystal shape, hardness, and the way the crystal breaks apart.

◆ Skills Objective

You will be able to:

- predict the shape of crystals when crushed into smaller pieces.

◆ Using the QX3 Microscope you Will...

Capture images of large and small salt crystals for comparison.

◆ Materials

QX3 microscope
rock salt crystals
metal spoons or small mallets
paper towels
goggles

◆ Safety Tips   *Review the safety guidelines in the front of your lab book.*

◆ Procedure

1. Place a chunk of rock salt on the stage platform of the QX3 microscope. Take a snapshot of the rock salt, and make a rough sketch of your sample in the Data Collection and Observations section.
2. Put on your goggles. Place the rock salt on a hard surface and cover the salt with a paper towel. Use the back of a metal spoon or a rock hammer to break the salt into smaller pieces.
3. Examine these smaller pieces with the QX3 microscope. Take a snapshot of these salt pieces, and make a sketch in the Data Collection and Observations section of the shapes you see.
4. Crush a few of these smaller pieces with the spoon. Repeat Step 3.

Name ______________________ Date __________ Class ______________

HOW SMALL DO THEY GET? *(continued)*

◆ Data Collection and Observations

Salt Crystal Size	Sketch
Large - rock salt	
Medium - after first breakage	
Small - after crushing	

◆ Analyze and Conclude

1. What would the crystals look like if you crushed them into such small pieces that you needed a microscope to see them?

____

____

◆ Going Further

Create a poster of the different sized salt crystals from this experiment, showing their similarity of structure. Be sure to label the poster with the appropriate labels and magnification.

Name ______________ Date ________ Class ______________

Mostly Cloudy

◆ Background

Chemical properties change when new substances form. But what specific kinds of changes should you look for? First, a gas might be produced. If the reaction occurs in a liquid, you may see the gas as bubbles. Second, a color change may signal that a new substance has formed. Third, a solid may appear when two solutions are mixed. A solid that forms from solution during a chemical reaction is called a precipitate. Finally, other kinds of observable changes in properties can also signal a chemical reaction. For example, hard marble forms a crumbly solid when it reacts with acid rain.

◆ Skills Objective

- Inferring

◆ Using the QX3 Microscope you Will...

Make a movie of a chemical reaction occurring.

◆ Materials

QX3 microscope
carbonated water
limewater
tap water
plastic cups
graduated cylinder
safety goggles
lab apron

◆ Safety Tips   *Review the safety guidelines in the front of your lab book.*

◆ Procedure

1. Put on your safety goggles and apron.
2. Pour about 5 mL of limewater into a plastic cup.
3. Pour an equal amount of plain water into another plastic cup.
4. Add about 5 mL of carbonated water to the plain water cup. Use the QX3 microscope in hand-held mode to make a movie of the carbonated water and plain water mixture.
5. Repeat Step 4 with the limewater cup.

Name ____________________ Date __________ Class ______________

MOSTLY CLOUDY *(continued)*

◆ Data Collection and Observations

Mixture	Observations
Carbonated water and plain water	
Carbonated water and limewater	

◆ Analyze and Conclude

1. In which cup do you think a chemical reaction occurred?

____

____

2. What evidence supports your inference?

____

____

◆ Going Further

Repeat the part of the experiment in which carbonated water is added to limewater. Begin recording a real-time movie at the same time that you add the carbonated water to the limewater. Continue recording until you no longer observe any reaction taking place. Review the movie to determine how long it took for the reaction to go to completion. What factors could you change that would affect how fast the reaction occurred?

Name ______________________ Date __________ Class ______________

P7 **DISCOVER**

Can You Speed Up or Slow Down a Reaction?

◆ Background

Chemical reactions don't all occur at the same rate. Some, like explosions, are very fast. Others, like the rusting of metal, are much slower. Also, a particular reaction can occur at different rates depending on the conditions. A reaction's speed depends in part on how easily the particles of the reactants can get together. If you want to make a chemical reaction happen faster, you need to get more reactant particles together more often. To slow down a reaction, you need to do the opposite—get fewer particles together less often.

◆ Skills Objective

- Inferring

◆ Using the QX3 Microscope You Will...

Make movies of the reaction of vitamin C with iodine at different temperatures.

◆ Materials

QX3 microscope
clear plastic cups
3 500 mL heat resistant beakers
solutions of vitamin C tablets and water at three different temperatures
tincture of iodine
safety goggles
lab apron

PHYSICAL SCIENCE

◆ Safety Tips

Review the safety guidelines in the front of your lab book.

◆ Procedure

1. Obtain about 125 mL each of three solutions of vitamin C and water—one at room temperature, one at about 75°C, and one chilled to between 5° and 10°C.
2. Add three drops of iodine solution to the room temperature container and stir with a clean spoon. Make a short movie of any reactions that occur.
3. Repeat Step 2 with each of the remaining vitamin C and water solutions. Compare changes you observe in the solutions.
4. Clean up your work area and wash your hands.

Name ______________________ Date __________ Class __________

CAN YOU SPEED UP OR SLOW DOWN A REACTION? *(continued)*

◆ Data Collection and Observations

Reaction Temperature	Observations
Room Temperature	
75ºC	
5-10ºC	

◆ Analyze and Conclude

1. What conclusion can you make about the effect of temperature on the reaction of iodine and vitamin C?

____

____

◆ Going Further

Review the movies that you made of each reaction. How long did it take for each reaction to be completed? Construct a graph showing the reaction times for each of the three temperatures tested.

Name ______________________ Date __________ Class ______________

P 8 DISCOVER

What Makes a Mixture a Solution?

◆ Background

If you stir table salt into water, the salt disappears. Water and salt form a solution—a well-mixed mixture. If you taste a salt solution, any sip tastes just as salty as the next. Unlike a suspension, a solution has the same properties throughout. Solutions and suspensions also differ in the size of their particles and the way the parts of the mixtures can be separated. Dissolved particles are much smaller than suspended particles. They do not settle out of solution, and they pass through a filter. However, salt can be separated from water by boiling. Letting the water evaporate also works.

◆ Skills Objectives

- Observing

◆ Using the QX3 Microscope you Will...

Examine the microscopic properties of different liquid mixtures.

◆ Materials

QX3 microscope
2 paper cups
water
plastic spoon
pepper
table salt

PHYSICAL SCIENCE

◆ Safety Tips   *Review the safety guidelines in the front of your lab book.*

◆ Procedure

1. Put about 50 or 60 mL of water into a plastic cup. Add a spoonful of pepper and stir well.
2. To a similar amount of water in a second cup, add a spoonful of table salt. Stir well.
3. Examine each mixture using the QX3 microscope. Take a snapshot of each, and compare the appearance of the two mixtures. Record your findings in the Data Collection and Observations section.

Name ______________________ Date __________ Class __________

WHAT MAKES A MIXTURE A SOLUTION? *(continued)*

◆ Data Collection and Observations

Mixture	Description	Solution or Suspension?
Pepper and water		
Salt and water		

◆ Analyze and Conclude

1. What is the difference between the two mixtures?

2. What other mixtures have you seen that are similar to pepper and water?

3. What other mixtures have you seen that are similar to table salt and water?

◆ Going Further

Design an experiment to separate mixtures of sand and water and sugar and water.

PHYSICAL SCIENCE

Name ______________________ Date __________ Class ______________

P9 SHARPEN YOUR SKILLS

Classifying

◆ Background

The idea of putting two different materials together to get the advantage of both comes from the natural world. Many synthetic composites are designed to imitate a common natural composite—wood. Wood is made of long fibers of cellulose, held together by another plant polymer called lignin. Cellulose fibers are flexible and can't support much weight. At the same time, lignin is brittle and would crack under the weight of the tree branches. But the combination of the two polymers makes a strong tree trunk.

◆ Skills Objective

- Classifying

◆ Using the QX3 Microscope You Will...

Capture images of natural and synthetic fibers.

◆ Materials

QX3 microscope
clothing
several fabric types (for example, linen, wool, rayon, cotton, polyester)

◆ Safety Tip

Review the safety guidelines in the front of your lab book.

PHYSICAL SCIENCE

◆ Procedure

1. Sit or stand where you have a clear view of the room you are in. Slowly sweep the room with your eyes, making a list of the objects you see. Do the same sweep of the clothes you are wearing.
2. Determine which items on your list are made (completely or partly) of natural fibers and which items on your list are made of synthetic polymers.
3. Examine a few fibers from each of the examples that your teacher has set out with the QX3 microscope. Take a snapshot of each. Identify which fibers are synthetic and which are natural.

Name ____________________ Date ________ Class ____________

CLASSIFYING *(continued)*

◆ Data Collection and Observations

Items in the Room	Polymers *(check if Yes)*

Clothing	Polymers *(check if Yes)*

Fiber Examples	Natural or Synthetic

◆ Analyze and Conclude

1. What percent of the items were not made with polymers?

____

◆ Going Further

Make a poster showing the key differences between natural and synthetic fibers.

PHYSICAL SCIENCE

Name ______________________ Date __________ Class ______________

P10 **REAL WORLD LAB**

Packaging with Polymers

◆ Background

Molecules of some organic compounds can hook together, forming larger molecules. A polymer is a large, complex molecule built from smaller molecules joined together. The smaller molecules, from which polymers are built, are called monomers. Polymers form when chemical bonds link large numbers of monomers in a repeating pattern. A polymer may consist of hundreds, or even thousands, of monomers.

◆ Skills Objectives

- Designing experiments
- Controlling variables
- Drawing conclusions

◆ Using the QX3 Microscope you Will...

Investigate the microscopic properties of different polymers.

◆ Materials

QX3 microscope
water
scissors
balance
tape
clock or timer
weights (or books)
thermometers
containers (beakers, trays, plastic cups)
iodine solution (1% solution)
hard-boiled eggs (optional)
polymers used in packaging (paper, Tyvek, plastic foam, ecofoam, cardboard, fabric, popcorn, sawdust, wood shavings, or plastic)

◆ Safety Tips

Review the safety guidelines in the front of your lab book.

PHYSICAL SCIENCE

Name ______________________ Date __________ Class ______________

PACKAGING WITH POLYMERS *(continued)*

◆ Procedure

1. Write a hypothesis about the ideal properties a polymer should have if it is to be used for packaging.
2. Examine each polymer with the QX3 microscope. Take a snapshot of the microscopic structure of each polymer.
3. Make a list of all the ways you can think of to test the properties of polymers. Think about the properties including, but not limited to, the following:
   - ability to protect a fragile object
   - reaction to water
   - heat insulation
   - reaction to iodine
   - appearance
   - strength
   - mass

   (**NOTE:** *Iodine turns a dark blue-black color when starch is present. Starch may attract insects or other pests.*)
4. Select a property that you wish to test. Choose a method that you think would be the best way to test that property.
5. Design a step-by step procedure for the test. Do the same for each of the other properties you decide to investigate. Be sure that you change only one variable at a time. Include any safety directions in your procedure.
6. Predict which polymers you think will perform best in each test you plan.
7. After your teacher has approved your procedure, perform the tests on a sample of each polymer.
8. Record your observations in the Data Collection and Observations section.

◆ Data Collection and Observations

Record your observations in the space below.

Hypothesis:

____

____

Test Design:

____

____

PHYSICAL SCIENCE

Name ______________________ Date __________ Class __________

PACKAGING WITH POLYMERS *(continued)*

Polymer:	Brief Description of Test 1	Brief Description of Test 2	Brief Description of Test 3	Brief Description of Test 4
Polymer A				
Polymer B				
Polymer C				

◆ Analyze and Conclude

1. Describe the similarities and differences that you discovered among your samples.

2. Review the different tests that you used. Which worked well? Are there any tests you would do differently if you were to do them another time?

3. Which polymer, or polymers, would you use to package some breakable items for mailing? Explain your reasons for this choice.

4. Which polymer, or polymers, would you not want to use? Why?

5. Tyvek costs more than paper. Ecofoam costs more than plastic foam. How would this information influence your decision on which material to use?

◆ Going Further

Create a poster that relates the microscopic structure of each polymer with its performance as a packing material.

PHYSICAL SCIENCE

Name ______________________ Date __________ Class ______________

P11 **DISCOVER**

Are They Steel the Same?

◆ Background

An alloy is a mixture made of two or more elements that has the properties of metal. In every alloy, at least one of the elements is a metal. Alloys are used much more than pure metals because they are generally stronger and less likely to react with air or water. You have seen iron objects rust when they are exposed to air and water. But forks and spoons are made of stainless steel and can be washed over and over again without rusting. Stainless steel is an alloy of iron, carbon, nickel, and chromium. It does not react as easily with air and water as iron does.

◆ Skills Objective

- Developing hypotheses

◆ Using the QX3 Microscope you Will...

Capture microscopic images of corroded surfaces.

◆ Materials

QX3 microscope
cut nail
wire mail
stainless steel bolt
paper towel
sealable plastic bag
saltwater solution

◆ Safety Tip

Review the safety guidelines in the front of your lab book.

◆ Procedure

1. Take a snapshot of a cut nail (low-carbon steel), a wire nail (high-carbon steel), and a stainless steel bolt with the QX3 microscope. Then wrap the nails and bolt together in a paper towel.
2. Place the towel in a plastic bag. Add about 250 mL of salt water and seal the bag.
3. After one or two days, remove the nails and bolt. Take a snapshot of each with the QX3 microscope. Note any changes in the metals.

PHYSICAL SCIENCE

Name ______________________ Date __________ Class ______________

ARE THEY STEEL THE SAME? *(continued)*

◆ Data Collection and Observations

Item	Observations
Cut Nail	
Wire Nail	
Bolt	

◆ Analyze and Conclude

1. What happened to the three types of steel?

____

____

2. Which one changed the most, and which one changed the least?

____

____

3. What do you think accounts for the difference?

____

____

PHYSICAL SCIENCE

◆ Going Further

Create a poster that shows the difference in the amount of corrosion between the three types of steel items. You can design an experiment to test the effect of protective coatings on metals that are easily corroded, and create a poster showing the results of your experiment.

Name ______________________ Date __________ Class ______________

P12 **DISCOVER**

Does It Get Wet?

◆ Background

Ceramics are hard, crystalline solids made by heating clay and other materials to high temperatures. Clay is made of very small mineral particles containing silicon, aluminum, and oxygen. Clay forms when the minerals in rock are broken down. Unheated clay also contains water. When a clay object is heated, much of the water present on its surface evaporates, and the particles of clay stick together. This process forms the hard ceramic pottery used for bricks and flowerpots. Once cooled, these materials have tiny spaces in their structure that absorb and hold water. If you grow a plant in this kind of pot, you can feel the moisture in the outer surface of the clay after you water the plant. When pottery is brushed with a layer of silicon dioxide and heated again, a glassy coating, called a glaze, forms. This glaze is shiny and waterproof.

◆ Skills Objective

- Inferring

◆ Using the QX3 Microscope you Will...

Capture microscopic images of porous and waterproof ceramic containers.

◆ Materials

QX3 microscope
glazed and unglazed flowerpots of the same size
sink or basin
water
balance

◆ Safety Tip  *Review the safety guidelines in the front of your lab book.*

◆ Procedure

1. Find the masses of a glazed pottery flowerpot and an unglazed one of similar size. Record both values. Take snapshots of their surfaces using the QX3 microscope in hand-held mode.
2. Place both pots in a basin of water for ten minutes.
3. Remove the pots from the water, and blot dry gently with paper towels.
4. Find and record the masses of both flowerpots again.
5. Calculate the percent of change in mass for each pot.

PHYSICAL SCIENCE

Name ______________________ Date __________ Class __________

DOES IT GET WET? *(continued)*

◆ Data Collection and Observations

Flowerpot	Initial mass	New mass
Glazed		
Unglazed		

Percent of change in mass:

$$\frac{\text{(new mass} - \text{initial mass)}}{\text{initial mass}} \times 100\% =$$

◆ Analyze and Conclude

1. Which pot gained the most mass?

____

____

2. What can you infer about the effect that glazing has on the pot?

____

____

PHYSICAL SCIENCE

Name ______________________ Date __________ Class ______________

P13 **DISCOVER**

How Slow Can It Flow?

◆ Background

You may be surprised to learn that the Earth's lithosphere can move. After all, you know that the lithosphere is made up of solid rock! In fact, the lithosphere is broken into a number of large pieces called plates. The plates completely cover the Earth's surface and even extend under the oceans. They plates move very slowly—at rates of several centimeters per year. That's about as fast as your fingernails grow! As the plates move, the continents also move, or "drift", over the Earth's surface.

◆ Skills Objective

You will be able to:

- form an operational definition of movement.

◆ Using the QX3 Microscope you Will...

Make a time-lapse movie of the movement of honey so that you can calculate its speed.

◆ Materials

QX3 microscope
spoon
plate
honey
masking tape
metric ruler
books or blocks
damp cloths or paper towels

◆ Safety Tip  *Review the safety guidelines in the front of your lab book.*

◆ Procedure

1. Put a spoonful of honey on a plate.
2. Using a ruler, place a piece of tape 2 cm away from the edge of the honey.
3. Place the plate on the stage platform of the QX3 microscope, and lift one side of the plate just high enough that the honey is visibly flowing.

PHYSICAL SCIENCE

HOW SLOW CAN IT FLOW? *(continued)*

4. Reduce the angle of the plate a small amount so that the honey appears to be barely moving. Prop up the plate at this angle, so that the tape is visible in the field of view. Use the metric ruler to measure the starting distance between the honey and the tape.
5. Begin recording a time-lapse movie at one-minute intervals. Use the time it takes for the honey to flow to the tape to calculate the speed of the honey.

◆ Data Collection and Observations

Starting Distance from Honey to Tape	Time for Honey to Reach the Tape

◆ Analyze and Conclude

1. How can you tell that an object is moving if it doesn't appear to be moving at first glance?

____

____

2. Can you think of some other examples of motion that are too slow to see?

____

____

PHYSICAL SCIENCE

◆ Going Further

Make some predictions about factors that could change the speed of a moving substance. Design an experiment to test your predictions. Use the QX3 microscope to determine if your predictions were accurate.

Name ____________________ Date __________ Class __________

P14 REAL WORLD LAB

Sticky Sneakers

◆ Background

Newton's first law of motion states that an object at rest will remain at rest. Also, an object that is moving at a constant velocity will continue moving at a constant velocity unless it is acted upon by an unbalanced force. The first part of this law is easy to observe. For example, if you place a book on your desk, the book won't move unless you push it. The second part of this law is less obvious than the first part. If you roll a marble across the floor, it will eventually stop. The marble stops because two unbalanced forces, friction and air resistance, slow it down. Friction is the force that two surfaces exert on each other when they rub against each other. In this case, the surface of the marble rubs against the floor's surface.

◆ Skills Objectives

You will be able to:

- form operational definitions of starting friction, forward-stopping friction, and sideways-stopping friction;
- measure the force required to overcome friction;
- control variables such as total mass.

◆ Using the QX3 Microscope you Will...

Capture images of magnified views of various sneaker surfaces.

◆ Materials

QX3 microscope
three or more different types of sneakers
spring scale, 20 N or 5 N, or force sensor
mass set
large paper clip
tape
balance

◆ Safety Tips

  *Review the safety guidelines in the front of your lab book.*

◆ Procedure

1. Sneakers are designed to deal with various friction forces, including these:
   - starting friction, which is involved when you start from a stopped position
   - forward-stopping friction, which is involved when you come to a forward stop
   - sideways-stopping friction, which is involved when you come to a sideways stop

PHYSICAL SCIENCE

Name ______________________ Date __________ Class ______________

STICKY SNEAKERS *(continued)*

2. Use the QX3 microscope to take snapshots of the different tread patterns on the bottom of each of the different sneakers.
3. Place each sneaker on a balance. Then put masses in each sneaker so that the total mass of the sneaker plus the masses is 1,000 g. Distribute the masses evenly inside the sneaker.
4. You will need to tape the paper clip to each sneaker and then attach a spring clip to the paper clip. To measure
   - starting friction, attach the paper clip to the back of the sneaker
   - forward-stopping friction, attach the paper clip to the front of the sneaker
   - sideways-stopping friction, attach the paper clip to the side of the sneaker
5. To measure starting friction, pull the sneaker backward until it starts to move. Use the 20 N spring scale first. If the reading is less than 5 N, use a 5 N scale. If using a force sensor, see your teacher for instructions. The force necessary to make the sneaker start moving is equal to the friction force. Record the starting friction force in the Data Collection and Observations section.
6. To measure either type of stopping friction, use the spring scale to pull each sneaker at a slow, constant speed. Record the stopping friction force in the Data Collection and Observations section.
7. Repeat Steps 4 through 6 for the remaining sneakers.

◆ Data Collection and Observations

Data Table

Sneaker	Starting friction (N)	Sideways-stopping friction (N)	Forward-stopping friction (N)
A			
B			
C			

PHYSICAL SCIENCE

◆ Analyze and Conclude

1. What are the manipulated and responding variables in this experiment? Explain.

____

____

Name ______________________ Date __________ Class ______________

STICKY SNEAKERS *(continued)*

2. Why is the reading on the spring scale equal to the friction force in each case?

____

____

3. Do you think that using a sneaker with a small amount of mass in it is a fair test of the friction of the sneakers? (Consider the fact that sneakers are used with people's feet inside them.) Explain your answer.

____

____

4. Draw a diagram that shows the forces acting on the sneaker for each type of motion.

5. Why did you pull the sneaker at a slow speed to test for stopping friction? For starting friction, why did you pull a sneaker that wasn't moving?

____

____

6. Which sneaker had the most starting friction? Which had the most forward stopping friction? Which had the most sideways stopping friction?

____

____

7. Can you identify a relationship between the type of sneaker and the type of friction you observed? What do you observe about the sneakers that would cause one to have better traction than another?

____

____

STICKY SNEAKERS *(continued)*

8. Wear a pair of your own sneakers. Start running and notice how you press against the floor with your sneaker. How do you think this affects the friction between the sneaker and the floor? How can you test for this variable?

____

____

____

◆ Going Further

Create a poster that illustrates sneaker surface types and their relation to the amount and type of friction they generate.

Name ______________________ Date __________ Class ______________

P15 **TRY THIS**

How Do Light Beams Behave?

◆ Background

In general, the wave model can explain many of the properties of electromagnetic radiation. However, some properties of electromagnetic radiation do not fit the wave model. Light has many of the properties of waves. But light can also act as though it is a stream of particles. When light passes through a polarizing filter, it has the properties of a wave. An ordinary beam of light has waves that vibrate in all directions. A polarizing filter acts as though it has tiny slits that are either horizontal or vertical. When light enters a polarizing filter, only some waves can pass through. The light that passes through is called polarized light.

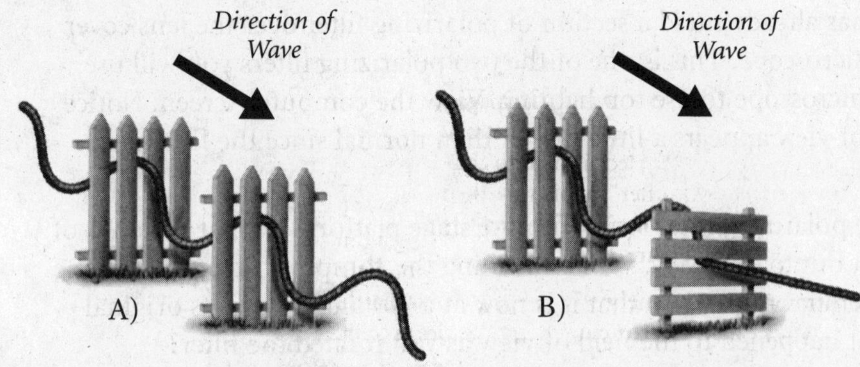

A Polarizing filter acts like the slate in a fence. (A) A fence with vertical slates allows only waves that vibrate up and down to pass through. (B) Vertical waves cannot pass through a fence, or filter, with horizontal slats.

◆ Skills Objective

- Drawing conclusions

◆ Using the QX3 Microscope you Will...

Make a movie showing the effect of using cross-polarized filters on the transmission of light.

◆ Materials

QX3 microscope fitted with one polarizing filter
2 plastic cups
water
pan or sink
slide projector
flashlight
polarizing filter strip

PHYSICAL SCIENCE

HOW DO LIGHT BEAMS BEHAVE? *(continued)*

◆ Safety Tip  *Review the safety guidelines in the front of your lab book.*

◆ Procedure

1. Fill two plastic cups with water. Slowly pour the water from the two cups into a sink. Aim the stream of water from one cup across the path of the water from the other cup.
2. How do the two streams interfere with each other?
3. Now darken a room and project a slide from a slide projector onto the wall. Shine a flashlight beam across the projector beam.
4. How do the two beams of light interfere with each other? What effect does the interference have on the projected picture?
5. Your teacher has already fitted a section of polarizing filter over the lens cover on the QX3 microscope. This is one of the two polarizing filters you will use. Set the QX3 microscope to use top lighting. View the computer screen. Notice that the field of view appears a little darker than normal since the filter is in place.
6. Now place the polarizing filter strip onto the stage platform so that the ends of the filter point out to each side. While watching the computer screen, hold one end of the filter and rotate it so that it is now at a 90° angle from its original position. What happened to the field of view as you rotated the filter?

◆ Data Collection and Observations

Experiment	Observations
Crossed water streams	
Crossed light beams	
Crossed polarizing filters	

Name ________________ Date ________ Class ________________

HOW DO LIGHT BEAMS BEHAVE? *(continued)*

◆ Analyze and Conclude

1. How is the interference between light beams different from that between water streams?

____

____

2. Does this activity support a wave model or a particle model of light? Explain.

____

____

◆ Going Further

Sprinkle a small amount of salt onto a dry microscope slide. Place the microscope slide with salt crystals on top of the polarizing filter strip on the stage platform of the QX3. Using the QX3 at 10X magnification and top lighting, view the salt crystals. Does the field of view appear black? If not, rotate the strip and the slide by 90°. When the field of view appears black, observe the salt crystals. Do the salt crystals appear to glow? Take a snapshot. Repeat this procedure using sugar crystals. Can you distinguish the salt crystals from the sugar crystals? Be sure to take snapshots and record your observations.

PHYSICAL SCIENCE

Name ______________________ Date __________ Class ______________

P16 **DISCOVER**

Are You Seeing Spots?

◆ Background

Have you ever wondered how a color TV screen works? A video signal is sent to a very specialized type of vacuum tube, known as a cathode-ray tube. A cathode-ray tube (CRT), or picture tube, is an electronic device that uses electrons to produce images on a screen. A CRT converts video signals into a pattern of light. At the back end of a CRT, there are three electron guns, one for each of the primary colors of light—red, blue, and green. The front end of a CRT is the screen that you see. The inside of the screen is coated with fluorescent materials, called phosphors, that glow when they are hit by an electron beam. The phosphors are arranged in clusters of three dots—one for each color. Each cluster is surrounded by dark space. The video signal is fed to the electron guns, causing each one to aim at the matching phosphor at the appropriate time. Your eyes combine the three colors to form all of the colors in the images you see.

◆ Skills Objectives

- Classifying

◆ Using the QX3 Microscope you Will...

Capture images of a CRT computer monitor screen or color television at various magnifications.

◆ Materials

QX3 microscope
color CRT monitor or color television

◆ Safety Tips

Review the safety guidelines in the front of your lab book.

◆ Procedure

1. Turn on a color television or computer monitor. Hold the QX3 microscope, in hand-held mode, up to the television or monitor screen.
2. Move the lens closer to and farther from the screen until you can see a clear image through it. What do you see within the image? Take a snapshot, and record your observations in the Data Collection and Observations section.
3. Repeat Step 2 at other magnifications on the QX3 microscope.

PHYSICAL SCIENCE

Name ______________________ Date __________ Class ______________

◆ Data Collection and Observations

Magnifications	Observations
10X	
60X	
200X	

◆ Analyze and Conclude

1. What three colors make up the images on the television or computer monitor screen?

____

____

2. How do you think these colors make up the wide range of colors you see on television or your computer monitor?

____

____

◆ Going Further

Create a poster showing how a television or computer monitor makes an image out of small dots of color.

To make ordering supplies easier, the Master Materials List cross-references by subject the materials needed for the lab activities. Although most materials are locally available, they can be purchased from Neo/SCI Corporation.

To Order or for Technical Assistance Call
1-800-526-6689
Fax 1-800-657-7523 www.neosci.com

Material Description	Quantity *(per class)*	Lab ID
Animal cell microscope slide, prepared	5	L5
Ants, large, black (not fireants)	20-30	L16
Baby food jar, small	5	L24
Bean, dried, kidney, lima, or black	5	L10
Beverages, some with caffeine, some without	varies	L22
Blackworms (Lumbriculus)	10	L22
Blood, human, prepared slide	5	L21
Bone, chicken or turkey leg, cooked	5	L17
Bread with no preservatives	5 slices	L2, L20
Breadcrumbs	1 can	L16
Breakfast cereal, several kinds	1/2 cup each	L20
Cactus, small potted	5	L23
Calculator	5	L6
Chicken wing, treated	5	L18
Chlorella culture	1	L9
Clay, 1" balls	5	L11
Construction paper, black	5 pieces	L16
Cork, prepared slide	5	L4
Corn seeds, soaked	20	L11
Cotton ball	5	L12
Coverslip, plastic	5	L4, L5, 24
Cup, paper	10	L25
Dissecting needle	5	L15
Dropper, plastic	5	L2, L4, L5, L9, L20, L22, L24
Elodea leaf	5	L5
Epinephrine hydrochloride	10 mg	L22
Feather	5	L14
Forceps	5	L5, L15, L16
Fruits	1 each	L20
Glass jar, large	5	L16
Hay, timothy	1 flake	L24
Hydra culture	1	L13
Ink pad	5	L7
Iodine solution	1	L20

TEACHER SUPPORT LIFE SCIENCE

Material Description	Quantity *(per class)*	Lab ID
Lettuce	5 leaves	L4
Newsprint	5	L3
Onion root tip cell microscope slide, prepared	5	L6
Owl pellet	5	L15
Pan, shallow, large	5	L16
Paper, white	30	L7
Paraffin specimen trough	5	L22
Paramecium culture	1	L9
Pea, dried, yellow or green	5	L10
Peanut, shelled	5	L10
Pencil, marking	5	L11, L16, L22
Pencils, colored	5 sets	L5, L6
Petri dish with cover, plastic	5	L11, L13
Photographs, newspaper	5	L3
Plastic bags, sealable	5	L2
Plate, plastic	5	L25
Pond water	100 mL	L4
Rice	1/2 cup	L20
Rock (10 cm in length, thin)	5 each	L17
Rubber band, large, thick	5	L16
Ruler, clear plastic metric	5	L1, L8, L10, L15
Scissors	5	L11, L12, L23
Scissors, dissecting	5	L18
Screen, wire or fiberglass	5 pieces	L16
Seeds, at least 15 different types	5 sets	L25
Seeds, sunflower	50	L8
Slide, microscope	5	L4, L5, L9, L20, L24
Soft drinks	1/2 cup each	L20
Soil, sandy	5 portions	L16
Sponge, synthetic kitchen	5	L12, L16
Sponge, natural	5 small	L12
Sugar, granulated	5 lb bag	L16
Tape, clear	1 roll	L16
Tape, masking	5 pieces	L11
Tape, packing	5 pieces	L2
Test tube	15	L20
Toothpick	5	L13
Towel, paper	10	L11, L18
Tray, dissecting	5	L18
Vegetables (starchy and nonstarchy)	1 of each	L20
Water, pond	1L	L24
Water, spring, non-carbonated	1/2 cup	L22

L1 React!

◆ Procedure Tips

- Have the subjects pretend that they are looking far off at a point in the distance. This will minimize their tendency to look at the light instead of to the side and past it.

◆ Time

20 minutes

◆ Data Collection and Observations

Individual measurements will vary depending upon individual differences and monitor size. Students should see a decrease in pupil diameter after three seconds of light exposure compared to its diameter upon first opening the eye.

◆ Analyze and Conclude

1. The pupil diameter should decrease when exposed to light.
2. Increased light intensity is the stimulus; it is an external stimulus.
3. Change in pupil size is the response.

L2 Please Pass the Bread

◆ Advance Planning

The day before the lab activity begins, obtain bread without preservatives.

◆ Time

Day 1: 15 minutes for setup
Days 2 – 5 (approximately): 5 minutes
On the day that mold growth is observed: 10 minutes to set up the QX3 microscope

◆ Data Collection and Observations

Students should begin noticing mold growth (fuzzy white patches) within 3-5 days, depending upon the temperature of the room. They should notice more mold growth sooner on the moistened bread slice than on the dry slice.

◆ Analyze and Conclude

1. Mold grows faster with moisture.
2. The variable was moisture.
3. The mold needed water, food (bread), and a place to grow.
4. Controlling variables means keeping all conditions the same except the one that the experimenter purposely changes. Experimenters need to be sure which variable caused a specific change.

◆ Going Further

Bread without any preservatives should mold faster than bread with added preservatives at comparable temperatures and growth conditions. Students should also conclude that mold grows faster in a warm and humid environment.

L3 Is Seeing Believing?

◆ Procedure Tip

- Make sure the students know how to set the magnification and lighting settings on the QX3 microscope before beginning.

◆ Time

15 minutes

◆ Data Collection and Observations

With the hand lens and microscope, students should see the individual dots of ink that make up the newspaper photograph. This will help them appreciate how the hand lens and microscope allow them to see objects too small to be seen with the naked eye.

◆ Analyze and Conclude

1. Students may say that with the hand lens and microscope, they can see that the black and grey shaded areas in the picture actually are made up of separate tiny dots of ink.
2. Microscopically, the paper is not smooth, but is rough and bumpy in texture.

◆ Going Further

All these materials have special surface coatings that make them "shiny" when observed using the "top" or reflective light of the QX3 microscope.

L4 Observing

◆ Procedure Tip

- A protist or algae culture from a biological supply house or a sample of water from a freshwater aquarium can be used in place of the pond water.

◆ Time

20 minutes

◆ Data Collection and Observations

The cork and lettuce drawing should show square to rectangular cells. Pond water drawings will vary. The number of cells that fit across one field of view will vary depending upon monitor size and cork or lettuce specimen.

◆ Analyze and Conclude

1. Students' drawings of cork cells should resemble Hooke's drawing in your textbook.
2. Leeuwenhoek called the organisms he saw "little animals" because they moved as animals move.

L5 A Magnified View of Life

◆ Advance Planning

Assemble all supplies. If the students are doing the Going Further activity, you'll need to have some methylene blue or iodine available for staining their skin cells. Elodea can be purchased at an aquarium fish store. Stains may be purchased from Neo/SCI Corporation or any other science supplier.

◆ Procedure Tip

- To avoid air bubbles being trapped under the coverslip of their wet-mount slides, you may wish to instruct the students to drop the coverslip onto the slide at a 45° angle so that all the air is pushed out from under the coverslip as it falls.

◆ Time

40 minutes

◆ Data Collection and Observations

Students should observe individual plant and animal cells under the microscope and draw diagrams that show their similarities and differences.

◆ Analyze and Conclude

1. Both kinds of cells have a cell membrane, nucleus, and such organelles as mitochondria and ribosomes.
2. Plant cells have a cell wall and chloroplasts, whereas animal cells do not.
3. The color is green; it comes from chloroplasts in the plant cells.
4. So you do not forget details.

◆ Going Further

Student should observe flattened, irregularly shaped cells, or cell clumps, some of which may show a dark stained nucleus.

L6 Multiplying by Dividing

◆ Advance Planning

Prepared slides can be purchased from Neo/SCI Corporation or any biological supply company.

◆ Procedure Tips

- Urge the students to review the photographs in Exploring the Cell Cycle in the textbook.
- A poster showing micrographs of each of the cell cycle and mitotic phases can also be purchased from a biological supply company for reference during this exercise.

◆ Time

40 minutes

◆ Data Collection and Observations

DATA TABLE

Stages of Cell Life	First Sample	Second Sample	Total Number
Interphase	43	46	89
Mitosis: Prophase	3	4	7
Metaphase	1	1	2
Anaphase	1	0	1
Telophase	0	1	1
		Total Number of Cells Counted	100

◆ Analyze and Conclude

1. The most likely answer is interphase.
2. Answers will vary depending on students' data. Answers for the sample data are: interphase, 641 minutes; prophase, 50 minutes; metaphase, 14 minutes; anaphase, 7 minutes; telophase, 7 minutes.
3. Based on the sample data, the amount of time spent in mitosis is 11 percent. Students' answers will vary depending on their data.

L7 What Do Fingerprints Reveal?

◆ Procedure Tip

- Help students recognize similarities and differences among the fingerprints by pointing out examples of whorls, loops, arches, and other standard features of fingerprints.

◆ Time

15 minutes

◆ Data Collection and Observations

By comparing a group's unlabeled fingerprint with its labeled fingerprints, students should be able to identify who made the unlabeled print.

◆ Analyze and Conclude

1. Each person's fingerprints are unique.

L8 How Do Living Things Vary?

◆ Procedure Tip

- Tell students that differences among seeds in their sample may be slight and hard to detect, so they should examine the seeds very carefully.

◆ Time

15 minutes

◆ Data Collection and Observations

Students should observe that the seeds in their sample differ in such traits as size, shape, color, or number of stripes.

◆ Analyze and Conclude

1. The seeds in each sample may differ in some traits and be similar in others.
2. Depending on the makeup of their sample, students may group together seeds that are similar in size, shape, color, number of stripes, or other traits.

L9 Feeding Paramecia

◆ Procedure Tips

- Another way to slow down the paramecia is to add one drop of a 2-3% solution of clear gelatin to the drop of culture on the slide.
- Make sure students wash their hands immediately after the activity.

◆ Time

15 minutes

◆ Data Collection and Observations

Student drawings should show the green *chlorella* cells inside the paramecium.

◆ Analyze and Conclude

1. Students should see green food vacuoles containing *chlorella* cells inside the paramecia. Students should conclude that paramecia are heterotrophs because they ingest the *chlorella.*
2. *Chlorella* behave like autotrophs because they do not seem to be ingesting food and are green like plants.

◆ Going Further

Generally, feeding paramecia will have engulfed 2 to10 *chlorella* cells, depending upon the organism's physiological state.

L10 The In-Seed Story

◆ Procedure Tips

- Obtain the beans and peas from a food store at least four days in advance of the activity.
- Soak the beans in water for two hours before the activity.
- Soak the peas for 24 hours.

◆ Time

15 minutes

◆ Data Collection and Observations

Students' answers will vary, depending upon the seed types used.

◆ Analyze and Conclude

1. The cotyledons are a food source for the young plant.
2. The seed coat protects the food source and the embryo until the seed germinates.
3. The embryo is the young plant that will grow out of the seed after germination. It will be photosynthetic after it emerges from the soil.

L11 Which Way Is Up?

◆ Advance Planning

Soak seeds in water for 24 hours prior to laboratory set-up.

◆ Procedure Tip

- Be sure that the students keep the petri dishes out for as little time as possible each day for recording observations and taking snapshots.

◆ Time

30 minutes for set up, plus a few minutes each day for a week

◆ Data Collection and Observations

Students' observations should note that roots begin to emerge and grow toward the earth over the observation period.

◆ Analyze and Conclude

1. Roots grew from the pointed tip of the seed, while the stem grew from the rounded part. The roots always grew downward, and the stems always grew upward, bending if necessary
2. Students should be able to explain any inconsistencies between their hypotheses and the evidence.
3. Plants usually grow toward light. Light was excluded so the direction of growth was affected only by gravity. The dark also simulated the underground environment in which seeds usually germinate.
4. Answers will vary. Students should realize that the results show that the direction of growth is influenced by gravity, not the direction in which the seeds are planted.

◆ Going Further

Students should conclude that all plants demonstrate a positive tropism in response to light—the emerging bean shoots grow towards the light source. Students should also observe that the emerging bean shoots display a negative tropism to gravity—they grew upwards. Roots, on the other hand, display a positive tropism to gravity—they grow downward!

L12 How Do Natural and Synthetic Sponges Compare?

◆ Advance Planning

Natural sponges and synthetic sponges must be obtained before class. Natural sponges can often be found in cosmetic departments or can be ordered from a biological supply house.

◆ Procedure Tip

- Direct students' attention to the pores on the surfaces of the sponges. Tell them that pores in a natural sponge are the openings of pathways through the sponge. Openings on a synthetic sponge are not connected by regular pathways.

◆ Time

20 minutes

◆ Data Collection and Observations

Students' diagrams should compare and contrast features of natural and synthetic sponges.

◆ Analyze and Conclude

1. Both have pores, hold liquid, and are soft.
2. They are different in material, color, texture, and shape.

L13 Hydra Doing?

◆ Advance Planning

You can order *Hydra* sp. from a biological supply house. If doing the Going Further activity, also order a culture of small water fleas (*Daphnia* sp.), and have plastic droppers available.

◆ Procedure Tip

- Guide students to observe characteristics of a cnidarian, in particular, the polyp body form represented by hydra.

◆ Time

25 minutes

◆ Data Collection and Observations

The normal movements cease when the tentacles are touched by the toothpick, and the hydra wraps its tentacles around the toothpick.

◆ Analyze and Conclude

1. It moves from place to place in a somersaulting fashion.

◆ Going Further

Students should observe the water flea held by the hydra's tentacles so that it cannot escape. After a while, the water flea will be drawn to hydra's mouth by the tentacles and slowly ingested.

L14 What Are Feathers Like?

◆ Advance Planning

Good sources of feathers are wooded areas, beaches, pet stores, bird sanctuaries, or biological supply houses. Fresh feathers should be frozen for 72 hours to kill organisms.

◆ Procedure Tip

- Try to have a variety of contour feathers. Point out the shaft and barbs of a feather before beginning the exercise.

◆ Time

15 minutes

◆ Data Collection and Observations

Student drawings should accurately reflect feather structure.

◆ Analyze and Conclude

1. The barbs do rejoin easily.
2. Because the barbs rejoin easily, this helps the birds smooth their feathers quickly to fly.

L15 Looking at an Owl's Leftovers

◆ Advance Planning

Order owl pellets from a biological supply company. If possible, obtain one for each student and a few extras.

◆ Procedure Tips

- Explain that the pellets have been decontaminated. Have reluctant students work with a partner and perform the roles of data collection and record keeping.
- It is helpful to break pellets into pieces and soak them in water to loosen the materials before beginning the dissection.

◆ Time

50 minutes

◆ Data Collection and Observations

Students should find a varying number of identifiable animal remains in their pellets.

TEACHER SUPPORT
LIFE SCIENCE

◆ Analyze and Conclude

1. Answers will vary. Students should explain that the number of each type of bone can help determine the number of animals eaten. For example, each skull represents one animal. Each pair of femurs represents one animal.
2. Combined data should give an estimate of the total number and type of animals in the pellets.
3. The estimated total of animals found in all pellets divided by the number of pellets dissected gives an average number of animals per pellet. Students can multiply this number by two to find the average number of animals eaten per day. Then, multiply the average number per day by 30 to find the average number of animals eaten per month.
4. Students may explain that they are less confident in their results because they will probably underestimate the number of animals eaten each month.

L16 One for All

◆ Advance Planning

CAUTION: *Avoid fire ants, as they are extremely aggressive. To check if a colony contains fire ants, tap on the mound with a small straw or twig. If the ants immediately swarm in large numbers, they are probably fire ants.*

Have students bring a glass jar to class a few days in advance. Large condiment jars work well. Ants can be collected from a colony in nature. Collect sufficient soil from the area close to the colony for students to use in their jars. Try to collect ants of various sizes from the colony. Dig up only a small part of the colony. Place the container with the ants you have collected in the refrigerator to slow the ants down. Keep ants chilled before adding to students' jars. Place 20-30 ants directly into students' jars so that students do not handle the ants. When finished, return all the ants to the refrigerator and then return then to their original colony.

◆ Procedure Tips

- Nylon screen can be substituted for the wire screen, as it is easier to cut with scissors.
- You may prefer to purchase an "ant farm" from a scientific supply house.

◆ Time

45 minutes on the first day, five minutes per day for two weeks after set up.

◆ Data Collection and Observations

Answers will vary. Student should notice that the soil changes over the course of the observations because the ants dig tunnels through it.

◆ Analyze and Conclude

1. Sample response: Some ants carried food to the food store, dug tunnels, and took items to the refuse pile.

2. Answers will vary depending on the behavior observed. The behaviors contribute to the building of a home, food storage, waste removal, care of offspring, and the protection of the entire colony.

3. Tunnels were dug through the soil over the course of the experiment. Ants must have caused these changes, since no other animals were present.

4. Sample response: Ants require soil in which they can dig and a source of food and water.

◆ Going Further

Ants have an elaborate system of communication, which includes tactile, gustatory, and olfactory signals. Gustatory interaction is accomplished through the oral exchange of food, a behavior pattern of critical importance to social organization in ants. Olfactory communication is achieved through the release of chemicals called pheromones, which permit ants to signal alarm, lay trails, and attract sister workers to new food sources.

L17 Hard as a Rock?

◆ Advance Planning

Make sure the chicken or turkey bone has been thoroughly cooked, cleaned of soft tissue, and then washed. If doing the Going Further activity, saw a second bone crosswise for students to examine using a small kitchen saw.

◆ Procedure Tip

- Remind students to observe as many characteristics as possible, such as size, shape, color, texture, composition, and strength.

◆ Time

10 minutes

◆ Data Collection and Observations

Observations will vary, but students should recognize that the rock is denser and stronger than the bone, and that the composition of bones and rocks is different.

◆ Analyze and Conclude

1. Students will probably say that bones are sometimes compared to rocks because both bones and rocks are hard.

2. Bone is not as dense as rock and has a definite structure. A bone is living, but a rock is not.

L18 A Look Beneath the Skin

◆ Advance Planning

- Use only fresh chicken wings. Wings should be used within 24 hours of purchase and must be stored in a refrigerator.
- Soak all wings in a solution of two parts household bleach and eight parts water for two hours before the lab. Rinse thoroughly with clear water to remove the bleach.
- Use disposable latex or nitrile gloves, or food handling gloves.
- Make sure students wear protective gloves throughout the lab.

◆ Procedure Tip

- Remind students to work slowly so they do not destroy parts of the wing before they have completely examined it.

◆ Time

30 minutes

◆ Data Collection and Observations

Students' drawing should accurately reflect the spatial relationships between the muscles, bones, tendons, and ligaments in the chicken wing.

◆ Analyze and Conclude

1. Up and down at the elbow, like a human elbow; hinge joint.
2. If students pull on the biceps, they bend the arm at the elbow. If they pull on the triceps, the arm straightens. The pulling represents muscle contraction.
3. Skeletal
4. Sample: Diagrams and snapshots allow you to compare structures of the arm, even though they are not visible at the same time.

L19 What Can You Observe About Skin?

◆ Procedure Tips

- Ask students to predict what they will observe through the QX3 microscope. Ask: What structures would you expect to see on the surface of your skin?

◆ Time

15 minutes

◆ Data Collection and Observations

Students should notice ridges, hairs, and pigmented areas on their skin. Following removal of the glove, they should also notice perspiration.

◆ Analyze and Conclude

1. The hand was covered with perspiration following removal of the glove.
2. It produced perspiration because the temperature inside the glove was higher than the temperature outside the glove. Perspiration is one of the functions of the skin that help to cool the skin down when it is too hot.

L20 Predicting the Presence of Starch

◆ Advance Planning

Assemble all supplies. Place each food sample in a labeled test tube.

◆ Procedure Tip

Set up stations and have students rotate in groups of three or four from station to station.

◆ Time

20 minutes

◆ Data Collection and Observations

Student predictions will vary depending upon food items present.

◆ Analyze and Conclude

Foods such as potatoes, pasta, rice, and cereal contain starch. Other fruits and vegetables may also contain small amounts of starch.

L21 What Kinds of Cells Are in Blood?

◆ Advance Planning

Obtain prepared human blood slides from a biological supply company.

◆ Procedure Tip

- Remind students to note the shapes and sizes of cells.

◆ Time

15 minutes

◆ Data Collection and Observations

Student sketches should accurately reflect the three distinct cellular components of blood.

◆ Analyze and Conclude

1. Students should describe three types of cells: round with a depressed center (red blood cells); irregularly shaped cells (white blood cells); and flat, fragmented bodies (platelets).

L22 With Caffeine or Without?

◆ Advance Planning

Purchase *Lumbriculus* (blackworms) and adrenaline (epinephrine) from a biological supply company. To prepare the adrenaline solution (about 0.01%), dissolve 10 mg epinephrine hydrochloride in 100 mL distilled water. Have available all other materials, including beverages with caffeine and "decaffeinated" beverages. Beverages should be diluted to neutralize pH levels. Suggested dilution is 1 mL beverage to 100 mL water.

◆ Procedure Tips

- Before the lab, remind students to treat the Lumbriculus with as much care as possible. Caution them not to taste any of the beverages. They should wash their hands thoroughly after the lab. Review the lab safety guidelines with your students.
- Demonstrate the proper procedure for moving Lumbriculus to the specimen trough.
- Possible beverage choices include cola or coffee, citrus soda or juice, caffeine-free cola or decaffeinated coffee.
- Students should use new Lumbriculus samples for Part 2. Exposing a single Lumbriculus to many different substances in quick succession would stress the organism and lead to erroneous data. In addition, residual amounts of the various test substances could remain in the Lumbriculus as it is exposed to new test substances.
- Students should count heartbeats as soon as they are able to view the blackworms. Viewing the lower half of the body, close to the tail will give the clearest view of the pulse.

◆ Time

40 minutes

◆ Data Collection and Observations

Normal pulse rate for *Lumbriculus*, depending upon the species, varies form 24 to 32 beats per minute.

Adrenaline and caffeine are stimulants and should cause the pulse to increase. Drinks without caffeine should not increase the pulse.

◆ Analyze and Conclude

1. A stimulant speeds up body processes.
2. Adrenaline caused an increase in the worm's pulse rate.
3. Yes.
4. Some students may infer that drinks without caffeine will have no effect on humans, but drinks with caffeine will cause increased heart rates and related changes. Other students may say that since humans and *Lumbriculus* are so different, the effect of caffeine on humans cannot be predicted based on this evidence.

◆ Going Further

Most "daytime" cough and cold remedies contain epinephrine derivatives and, thus, are stimulants increasing pulse rate. Some "nighttime" remedies contain additional depressants that slow pulse rate.

L23 Desert Survival

◆ Advance Planning

Obtain enough small potted cactus plants for several class groups from a nursery.

◆ Procedure Tips

- Divide the class into small groups and provide a separate cactus plant for each group.
- Use cactus varieties with narrow, tube-shaped or flat segments that will be easy for students to snip through with scissors.

◆ Time

10 minutes

◆ Data Collection and Observations

Observations will vary, but students should note the tough outer skin with a waxy cuticle and the fleshy moist tissue inside the cactus.

◆ Analyze and Conclude

1. Students should observe that unlike most other plants, cactuses have sharp spines or other projections, not flat, wide leaves, and they also have a waxy outer covering. The inside of a cactus is fleshy and moist.
2. The lack of wide, flat leaves and the waxy outer covering help conserve water in the hot, dry desert; the fleshy inner core stores moisture for the plant.

L24 Change in a Tiny Community

◆ Advance Planning

- The day before students will begin the lab, prepare a hay solution by adding a small amount of hay (preferably timothy hay) for each liter of hot water. Let the hay soak overnight, then strain the hay from the solution.
- Collect a sample of pond water.
- Ask students to help you collect clean baby-food jars.
- Collect field guides and other sources showing the types of microscopic organisms found in ponds.

◆ Procedure Tip

- Instead of pond water, use water from a freshwater aquarium or add a commercially prepared culture of microorganisms.

◆ Time

Day 1: set up community; 15 minutes
Days 3, 6, and 9: examine community; 20 minutes each day

◆ Data Collection and Observations

Individual observations will vary.

◆ Analyze and Conclude

1. Answers will vary. Students can usually expect to see a variety of microorganisms, including the three pictured.
2. After one or two days, the solution may become cloudy as bacteria and other microorganisms multiply. Small protists may appear early, followed by larger protists, such as green algae, paramecia, and amoebas. Tiny animals, such as water fleas and rotifers, may be visible toward the end of the sequence.
3. Abiotic factors include the amount of light received, the temperature of the water, and the space available for the populations. Biotic factors include predation of some organisms by other organisms. As smaller organisms multiplied, they provided a growing food supply for larger organisms, which could in turn increase in numbers as well.
4. The organisms were already in the hay solution or pond water, are offspring of those original organisms, or developed from fertilized eggs in the hay solution or pond water.
5. Answers may vary. Some students may say the picture of the model community was complete because they used a valid method of taking samples and made logical inferences and generalizations. Other students may say the picture was incomplete because only three small samples were taken on just three occasions, revealing only a small percentage of the organisms living in the community.

◆ Going Further

Since the experimental setup should mimic the quiet waters of a pond's waterline, students should place a small amount of collected bottom sediment with water in a plastic container. Allowing the water in the container to freeze, and then thawing it, could represent winter and spring conditions. Allowing the water in the jar to evaporate, and then adding more water (simulating rains), could represent summer and fall conditions. In either case, microlife population numbers and types will be affected, as various forms emerge from cysts and egg cases and other protective coverings following significant seasonal changes in water temperature and/or microhabitat.

L25 How Much Variety is There?

◆ Advance Planning

Use a mixture of at least ten types of seeds for Cup A and four or five types for Cup B.

◆ Procedure Tip

- If the students have trouble holding the QX3 microscope still for snapshots in hand-held mode, they can place one seed type at a time on the stage platform for a snapshot.

◆ Time

20 minutes

◆ Data Collection and Observations

Student answers will vary based on the samples provided in Cups A and B. They should be able to calculate the class average number of seed types in the rainforest and deciduous forest.

◆ Analyze and Conclude

1. The tropical rain forest has a greater variety of trees than the deciduous forest.
2. The wider variety of tree species supports a wider variety of other organisms that depend on the trees for habitat and food.

To make ordering supplies easier, the Master Materials List cross-references by subject the materials needed for the lab activities. Although most materials are locally available, they can be purchased from Neo/SCI Corporation.

To Order or for Technical Assistance Call
1-800-526-6689
Fax 1-800-657-7523 **www.neosci.com**

Material Description	**Quantity** *(per class)*	**Lab ID**
Balance	1	E7
Bowls, plastic, small	10	E18
Calcite samples	5	E2
Candle	5	E4
Coal, lignite	5	E16
Conglomerate sample	5	E5
Construction paper, black	30	E3
Coquina samples	5	E9
Coverslip, plastic	5	E17
Cup, paper	5	E12
Dropper, plastic	5	E9, E13, E17
Epsom salt	1 box	E3
Gneiss sample	5	E7
Granite sample	5	E6, E7
Hydrochloric acid, dilute	50 mL	E9
Index card	5	E1
Lamp, incandescent	1	E1
Limestone samples	5	E9
Marble sample	5	E5
Matches	5	E4
Obsidian samples	5	E6, E10
Pan, shallow	5	E3, E7
Paper, graph (1mm or 2mm ruled)	5 sheets	E13
Penny, copper	5	E2, E5
Petri dish with cover, plastic	10	E1, E13, E14, E17
Phenyl salicylate (salol)	1 container	E4
Pitchers	2	E3
Plastic wrap	10 pieces	E11, E18
Plate, plastic	5	E11
Pond water	100 mL	E17
Quartz samples	5	E2
Pumice samples	5	E10
Rocks containing fossils	5	E15
Rubber bands	10	E18

Material Description	Quantity *(per class)*	Lab ID
Ruler, clear plastic metric	5	E1
Sand, beach (from 2 areas)	5 tsp each	E14
Sandstone sample	5	E7
Shale sample	5	E7
Slide, microscope	10	E4, E17
Sodium chloride	1 box	E3
Soil	5 portions	E12, E13
Spoon, plastic	5	E4, E13, E14
Steel wool	5 pads	E11
Talc samples	5	E2
Tongs	5	E4
Toothpick	5	E12, E13
Towel, paper	10	E12

E1 Speeding Up Evaporation

◆ Procedure Tips

- Be sure that the students use approximately equal-sized water drops for the three observations and that the QX3 microscope is set at 10X magnification.
- Caution students to be careful when handling a lamp, because the bulb gets hot and can explode if splashed with water.

◆ Time

30 minutes

◆ Data Collection and Observations

Students should find that both heat and fanning decrease the time necessary to evaporate the water droplet. Individual answers will vary due to differences in initial size of water droplets.

◆ Analyze and Conclude

1. Answers will vary. Some students may have foreseen the results correctly in each case and confirmed their hypothesis through the experiment.
2. Factors that increase the rate of evaporation of water include exposure to a heat source and exposure to wind.
3. Sample response: how quickly a puddle dries in the sun or wind. Hypotheses are based on information gathered through study or experience, whereas guesses are based only on feelings.

E2 Classifying

◆ Procedure Tips

- Divide students into pairs, pairing students of different abilities.

◆ Time

10 minutes

◆ Data Collection and Observations

A fingernail scratches talc, but not calcite or quartz. A penny scratches talc and calcite, but not quartz. Students may record visual observations of the minerals' appearances also.

◆ Analyze and Conclude

1. Quartz could not be scratched with either the fingernail or the penny.
2. The minerals, in order of increasing hardness, are: talc, calcite, and quartz.

E3 Crystal Hands

◆ Advance Planning

Prepare ahead of time supersaturated solutions of salt and Epsom salts by adding those substances to separate pitchers of hot water, allowing the water to cool, and then adding more salt or Epsom salts.

◆ Procedure Tips

- To simplify the activity, also pour the solutions into the shallow pans ahead of time, filling each to a depth of 1-2 cm.
- Provide a place for the hand prints to dry overnight.

◆ Time

15 minutes the first day; ten minutes for observation a day later

◆ Data Collection and Observations

The water in the solutions will evaporate overnight, leaving solid crystals as hand prints. Students will observe that the halite crystals are cubic, while the Epsom salts crystals are orthorhombic, or prism-shaped.

◆ Analyze and Conclude

Which hand prints have more crystals can vary, depending on the conditions of the experiment.

E4 How Does the Rate of Cooling Affect Crystal Growth?

◆ Advance Planning

Obtain salol (phenyl salicylate) from a drugstore or chemical supply house.

◆ Procedure Tips

- Students should wear goggles to make sure they do not get salol in their eyes.
- Caution students not to overheat the slide, especially the one placed on ice because it might break. Moving the slide from side to side over the flame will prevent overheating.
- Keep the slides on which the salol has hardened for remelting by other classes.

◆ Time

15 minutes

◆ Data Collection and Observations

The crystals that form on the two slides will be of different sizes. On the first slide, the crystals should be larger, because of the slower cooling. On the second slide, the crystals should be smaller, because of the more rapid cooling.

◆ Analyze and Conclude

1. The first sample should have larger crystals.
2. The crystals formed by rapid cooling should have small crystals.

◆ Going Further

Student results should confirm that the rate of cooling affects crystal size. Longer cooling rates (slow loss of temperature over time) allow for formation of larger crystals; shorter cooling rates (fast loss of temperature over time) produce smaller-sized crystals.

E5 How are Rocks Alike or Different?

◆ Advance Planning

Obtain marble and conglomerate samples.

◆ Procedure Tip

- If you have only a few samples of each kind of rock, pair samples of about the same size and place pairs at strategic places around the classroom. Then invite students to examine the pair closest to them.

◆ Time

10 minutes

◆ Data Collection and Observations

Individual student observations will vary.

◆ Analyze and Conclude

1. Students should discover that marble has a "sugary," crystalline texture that can easily be seen. Conglomerate has a rough texture and is clearly composed of small rocks and other materials, such as sand and shells. Both marble and conglomerate vary in color.

E6 How do Igneous Rocks Form?

◆ Procedure Tip

- If samples of granite and obsidian are unavailable, use any two igneous rocks with similar composition, but obviously different textures, such as gabbro and basalt, or diorite and andesite.

◆ Time

10 minutes

◆ Data Collection and Observations

Granite and obsidian are very similar in composition, but have different textures because granite forms from magma and obsidian forms from lava. Students should observe that the granite has coarse-grained crystals, while the glassy obsidian has no crystals.

◆ Analyze and Conclude

1. Students should infer that the granite formed as magma slowly cooled deep beneath Earth's surface, while the obsidian formed as lava cooled quickly on the surface.

E7 Rock Absorber

◆ Advance Planning

Obtain sandstone and shale samples of at least 25 g mass each.

◆ Procedure Tips

- Samples need to be at least 25 g to show a significant change in mass.
- If there are not enough samples for every student, divide the class into small groups.
- Make sure the pans will hold enough water to totally immerse the samples provided.
- Set up one or more balances in a central location so students can take each sample to a balance to find its mass.

◆ Time

15 minutes for setup; 10 minutes the next day

◆ Data Collection and Observations

Students should observe that sandstone is rough and coarse-grained, while shale is smooth and fine-grained. The mass of each rock will vary depending on the samples used.

◆ Analyze and Conclude

1. Students should find that the mass of the shale changes little or not at all after being submerged overnight, while the mass of the sandstone increases substantially.
2. They should conclude that sandstone has spaces between particles to absorb water, while shale does not.

E8 How Do Patterns of Gneiss and Granite Compare?

◆ Advance Planning

Obtain gneiss and granite samples.

◆ Procedure Tip

- Since the color of both gneiss and granite varies, try to obtain samples of each that are of similar color in order to focus the students' attention on the more relevant characteristic of texture.

◆ Time

15 minutes

◆ Data Collection and Observations

Students should observe that both granite and gneiss are coarse-grained. In granite, the grains are more angular than those in gneiss. The grains in gneiss appear flattened and more compact. Students' sketches should reflect these differences.

◆ Analyze and Conclude

Answers may vary. A typical answer might suggest that tremendous pressure and heat could cause such a change to occur.

E9 What Can You Conclude From the Way a Rock Reacts to Acid?

◆ Advance Planning

Assemble supplies. Coquina is a clastic rock, composed of shells and shell fragments. A fossil shell can be used as an alternative. Coral is not recommended for this activity because of conservation concerns.

◆ Procedure Tips

- Caution students that the dilute (5%) hydrochloric acid needs to be handled with extreme care. You could use white vinegar, which is a weak acid, in place of the dilute HCl, though the effect will not be as strong.

◆ Time

15 minutes

◆ Data Collection and Observations

Students should observe that hydrochloric acid fizzes where it comes in contact with limestone and coquina.

◆ Analyze and Conclude

1. The color and texture of the rocks will vary depending on the samples used.
2. Hydrochloric acid fizzes where it comes in contact with limestone and coquina, thus testing positive for the mineral calcite.
3. Students should conclude that coral also contains calcite in its composition.

◆ Going Further

Other calcite containing rocks include dolomite and marble, among others.

E10 What are Volcanic Rocks Like?

◆ Procedure Tip

- Help students with the correct pronunciations of pumice (PUHM is) and obsidian (ob SID ee un).

◆ Time

5-10 minutes

◆ Data Collection and Observations

The obsidian is smooth and glassy, whereas the pumice is rough and porous.
CAUTION: *Advise students to handle the obsidian with care because it sometimes has sharp edges that can cut the skin.*

◆ Analyze and Conclude

1. The lava that produced the pumice had more gas (air) in it than the lava that produced the obsidian. Obsidian formed when lava cooled very quickly.

E11 Rusting Away

◆ Procedure Tip

- Don't use steel-wool pads that contain soap. To cut down on the cost of materials, cut each pad in half.

◆ Time

5 minutes for setup; 5 minutes a few days later

◆ Data Collection and Observations

The moistened steel wool crumbles and stays compacted, while the new piece will spring back to the original shape. A new steel wool pad appears shiny and metallic, while the moistened one appears red and crumbly and is no longer shiny.

◆ Analyze and Conclude

1. The steel wool pad would eventually fall apart and rust away.

2. Like the oxidation of rock, the steel wool becomes crumbly and turns reddish.

E12 What is Soil?

◆ Advance Planning

Collect the soil sample at least a day in advance. You can collect the soil from your local area or buy commercial topsoil.

◆ Procedure Tip

- Provide each student with about 50 mL of soil in a paper cup. Advise students to pour the sample onto a paper plate or towel for examination.

◆ Time

15 minutes

◆ Data Collection and Observations

Answers will vary based on the soil sample examined.

◆ Analyze and Conclude

1. Answers may vary. A typical answer might suggest that soil is a mixture of different substances, including sand, clay, rock particles, and material derived from living things.

TEACHER SUPPORT
EARTH SCIENCE

E13 Getting to Know the Soil

◆ Advance Planning

Collect soil at least a day in advance, and make sure the soil is relatively dry. Use a balance to prepare individual samples of 20-30 grams each.

◆ Procedure Tip

- Students can observe both wet and dry soil under the QX3 microscope. Advise students to leave the wet soil in the petri dish.

◆ Time

40 minutes

◆ Data Collection and Observations

Answers will vary depending on the soil sample provided.

◆ Analyze and Conclude

1. Students should notice various characteristics, including color and texture.
2. From observations of particle size, texture, and how water changed the sample, students should be able to estimate what proportions of the sample are sand, clay, silt, and organic material.
3. Answers will vary. Students should support their inferences with evidence from their observations.
4. Questions will vary. Sample questions: What percentage of the soil is composed of humus? What is the texture of the soil?

E14 What Can Be Learned from Beach Sand?

◆ Advance Planning

Collect sand from nearby beaches if practical; otherwise, obtain two commercially available kinds of sand.

◆ Procedure Tip

- Suggest that students avoid mixing the two samples by completely removing the first sample before examining the second.

◆ Time

15 minutes

◆ Data Collection and Observations

Students should observe differences in the two samples, such as differences in particle shape, size, color, and texture. Specific differences will depend on the samples used.

◆ Analyze and Conclude

1. Questions will vary. Sample questions: Is beach sand a result of erosion? How is beach sand deposited? What causes differences in samples of beach sand collected at different places?

E15 What's in a Rock?

◆ Procedure Tip

- Divide students into small groups, and give each group a fossil-bearing rock.
- Then explain that each student should examine the rock, make a sketch, and write answers before discussing the rock with other group members.

◆ Time

10 minutes

◆ Data Collection and Observations

Sketches and descriptions will vary based on the sample provided.

◆ Analyze and Conclude

1. Most students should recognize that the rock contains one or more fossils.
2. A typical explanation of how the fossils formed might suggest that an organism fell into sediments and later solidified.

E16 What's in a Piece of Coal?

◆ Procedure Tip

- Lignite—the second stage of coal formation after peat—is the only form of coal that may contain recognizable plant remains.

◆ Time

10 minutes

◆ Data Collection and Observations

Student responses may vary depending on the sample observed.

◆ Analyze and Conclude

1. The lignite's texture, layers, and fossils (if present) can be seen more clearly with the QX3 microscope. If fossils are visible, students should be able to infer that coal is made of plant remains.

◆ Going Further

Models might include trapping materials such as leaves or pieces of colored paper in layers of soft material such as clay or soil, and then compressing the materials under heavy weights. Over time, heat and pressure change the materials into hydrocarbons.

E17 What's in Pond Water?

◆ Advance Planning

Collect water from a local pond, making sure you obtain some bottom mud and suspended particles.

◆ Procedure Tip

- As an alternative to collecting pond water, you can prepare a hay infusion or use prepared slides.

◆ Time

20 minutes

◆ Data Collection and Observations

Students should see larger organisms at 10X magnification and a greater variety of organisms at 60X magnification.

◆ Analyze and Conclude

1. Students could use movement or the consumption of smaller particles as criteria for deciding whether items are alive. Students should recognize that pond water contains a variety of living and nonliving things.

E18 Modeling a Humid Climate

◆ Procedure Tip

- Have students find their own locations to place the bowls or, to save time, choose the locations yourself.

◆ Time

10 minutes for set-up, 5 minutes for later observation

◆ Data Collection and Observations

Students will observe more water drops on the plastic wrap of the warm bowl than on the plastic wrap of the cool bowl.

◆ Analyze and Conclude

1. More water vapor is present in the air of warm climates because solar energy warms water, causing it to evaporate into the air.

◆ Going Further

Students should conclude that the rate of evaporation (i.e., water loss over time) is greatest at higher temperatures under similar (i.e., room humidity) conditions.

E19 What Story Can Tree Rings Tell?

◆ Advance Planning

Collect several stem sections from shrubs or small trees that have died if doing the Going Further activity.

◆ Procedure Tips

- Make a photocopy of the tree ring photo in your textbook and enlarge it. Students can label the thick and thin tree rings on the photocopy. If possible, provide students with cross-sections of tree trunks to examine.

◆ Time

10 minutes

◆ Data Collection and Observations

Students should observe that tree rings are not all the same thickness.

◆ Analyze and Conclude

1. Students might infer that temperature and precipitation affect the thickness of tree rings. Students should infer that the relative thickness of tree rings tells about weather conditions in the past.

To make ordering supplies easier, the Master Materials List cross-references by subject the materials needed for the lab activities. Although most materials are locally available, they can be purchased from Neo/SCI Corporation.

Material Description	Quantity (*per class*)	Lab ID
Balance	1	P10, P12, P14
Balloon	5	P1
Basin or pan	1	P12, P15
Beaker, 250 mL	5	P4
Beakers, 500 mL	3	P7, P10
Bolt, stainless steel	5	P11
Bowl, glass	5	P2
Candles, wax	5	P1
Cards, playing	1 deck	P1
Cathode ray tube (television, computer monitor)	1	P16
Clock or timer	1	P10
Coins	10	P1
Construction paper, black	5 pieces	P3, P4
Cups, paper	10	P8
Cups, plastic	10	P6, P7, P10, P15
Eggs, hard-boiled (optional)	12	P10
Fabric samples, such as linen, wool, rayon, cotton, polyester	1 each	P9
Flashlight	5	P15
Flowerpot, glazed	1	P12
Flowerpot, unglazed	1	P12
Fluorite crystals	5 tsp	P3
Foil, aluminum	5 pieces	P1
Force sensor (optional)	5	P14
Graduated cylinder, 10 mL	5	P6
Graduated cylinder, 100 mL	5	P4
Halite crystals	5 tsp	P3
Honey	100 mL	P13
Hot plate	1	P4, P7
Iodine, tincture of	1 bottle	P7, P10
Limewater	25 mL	P6
Mallet or metal spoon	5	P5
Mass set	5	P14
Nail, cut	5	P11

Material Description	Quantity (*per class*)	Lab ID
Nail, wire	5	P11
Paper clip, large	5	P1, P14
Pencil	5	P1
Pencil, marking	5	P4
Penny, copper, dated 1983 or later	5	P2
Pepper, ground	5 tsp	P8
Petri dish with cover, plastic	10	P4
Plastic bags, sealable	5	P11
Plate, paper or plastic	5	P13
Polarizing filter strip	5	P15
Polymers, packaging (such as Tyvek, paper, ecofoam, cardboard, popcorn, wood shavings, plastic)	1 of each	P10
Potassium iodide crystals	5 tsp	P3
Rocks, small	5-10	P1
Ruler, clear plastic metric	5	P2, P13
Sandpaper, fine	5 pieces	P2
Scissors	5 pairs	P10
Slide projector	1	P15
Sneakers, at least 3 different pairs	1 pair each	P14
Sodium chloride, granulated	10 Tbsp	P4, P8, P11
Sodium chloride, rock	5 pieces	P5
Sodium iodide crystals	5 tsp	P3
Spoon, plastic	5	P3, P4, P8, P13
Spring scale, 20N or 5N	5	P14
Tape, clear	1 roll	P10
Tape, duct	1 roll	P14
Tape, masking	5 pieces	P13
Thermometer	5	P10
Towel, paper	10	P5, P11, P13
Tray	5	P10
Vials, with water	5	P1
Vinegar	500 mL	P2
Vitamin C tablet	5	P7
Water, carbonated	25 mL	P6
Weights or books	several	P10

P1 What Properties Help You Sort Matter

◆ Procedure Tip

- Give each group samples of the ten objects to classify. Encourage students to think of original or interesting ways to classify objects.

◆ Time

15 minutes

◆ Data Collection and Observations

Answers will vary.

◆ Analyze and Conclude

1. Students may have grouped their objects according to shared properties. Another way to classify objects is by function. Students should identify the reasoning behind the groupings.

P2 Observing

◆ Procedure Tip

- A protist or algae culture from a biological supply house or a sample of water from a freshwater aquarium can be used in place of the pond water.

◆ Time

20 minutes

◆ Data Collection and Observations

The cork and lettuce drawing should show square to rectangular cells. Pond water drawings will vary. The number of cells that fit across one field of view will vary depending upon monitor size and cork or lettuce specimen.

◆ Analyze and Conclude

1. Students' drawings of cork cells should resemble Hooke's drawing in your textbook.
2. Leeuwenhoek called the organisms he saw "little animals" because they moved as animals move.

P3 Crystal Shapes

◆ Procedure Tip

- If your classroom has black desktops, students can pour their crystal samples into plastic petri dishes or onto colorless plastic wrap and use their desks as a viewing background with the QX3 microscope in hand-held mode.

◆ Time

15 minutes

◆ Data Collection and Observations

Student drawings will vary, but should reflect the crystal structure of the sample.

◆ Analyze and Conclude

1. Students will find that the crystals of a single compound have the same general shape, though they may differ somewhat in size.
2. Crystals of one compound may differ in shape from those of other compounds, but may look similar to still others.

P4 Shape Up!

◆ Advance Planning

Heat tap water to 80°C in large (1000 mL) beakers on hot plates from which students can obtain their portions.

◆ Procedure Tip

- The petri dishes should be left undisturbed while evaporation takes place to grow well-formed crystals.

◆ Time

30 minutes the first day and 15 minutes for observations the next day

◆ Data Collection and Observations

Crystals of sodium chloride will reform—some smaller than the original crystals, but having the same shape.

◆ Analyze and Conclude

1. The solid sodium chloride was no longer visible. It dissolved in water because the positive sodium ions and negative chloride ions separated, moving freely in solution.
2. The crystals look like cubes or rectangular solids. Some students may say the crystals look like boxes stacked on one another. Some crystals have an "x" pattern on their surfaces.
3. In both cases the crystals were white and cubic-shaped. Some new crystals may be of different sizes from those in Step 2 and exhibit the "x" pattern on their surfaces.

4. Ionic crystals have a definite structure. Yes. The sodium and chloride ions alternate in a three-dimensional cubic pattern.

5. Yes. You could predict that other ionic compounds will always form crystals having a specific shape.

◆ Going Further

Students should conclude that temperature does not affect crystal structure, but does affect the rate of crystal formation. Warmer temperatures favor increased solubility. Warmer solutions hold more solutes, such as sodium chloride, and thus re-crystallize faster than cooler solutions.

P5 How Small Do They Get?

◆ Procedure Tips

- As an alternative to covering the crystals with a paper towel, students can place the crystals in plastic sandwich bags.
- Small wooden mallets may work better than spoons for larger crystals.
- Remind students to wear lab goggles to prevent flying salt particles form going into their eyes.

◆ Time

12 minutes

◆ Data Collection and Observations

When crystals are broken or crushed, smaller crystals with the same shape are formed.

◆ Analyze and Conclude

1. The crystals would be shaped the same, like a cube, only much smaller.

P6 Mostly Cloudy

◆ Advance Planning

To make limewater, dissolve solid lime (calcium hydroxide, available at garden centers) in water until no more solid will dissolve. Filter the solution. **CAUTION:** *Wear safety goggles.*

◆ Procedure Tip

- Be sure that the students perform each experiment separately, so that they can record both for comparison.

◆ Time

15 minutes

◆ Data Collection and Observations

The reaction in the limewater cup will produce a white precipitate (calcium carbonate). As it settles, it will form a layer on the bottom of the cup. There will be no reaction in the plain water cup.

◆ Analyze and Conclude

1. There was a chemical reaction in the limewater cup.

2. The evidence for this is the white precipitate.

P7 Can You Speed Up or Slow Down a Reaction?

◆ Advance Planning

Prepare the vitamin C solution by crushing 1 tablet for every 480 mL of water. Each group will need 120 mL of the solution at each temperature. Pour one-third of the prepared solution into each beaker. Leave one at room temperature, chill one in an ice water bath, and heat the third in the beaker to about 75°C on a hot plate. Do not boil.

◆ Procedure Tip

- Caution students to avoid spills and splashes—iodine can stain skin and clothing.

◆ Time

15 minutes

◆ Data Collection and Observations

Vitamin C reacts with iodine and turns it colorless.

◆ Analyze and Conclude

1. At higher temperatures, the vitamin C and iodine react faster.

◆ Going Further

Student data should conclude that higher temperatures always increase the rate of an individual reaction. In this reaction, the yellow-brown iodine-colored solution will turn colorless most quickly at 75°C and most slowly at 10°C. Individual student results will vary due to tablet potency. Student bar graphs should show that the rate of reaction (elapsed time) increased as temperature decreased. A rule of thumb is that the rate of a reaction doubles with each increase of 10°C.

P8 What Makes a Mixture a Solution?

◆ Procedure Tip

- Remind students to wash the spoon before making their second mixture.

◆ Time

10 minutes

◆ Data Collection and Observations

The pepper will not dissolve in water (suspension), but the table salt will dissolve (solution).

◆ Analyze and Conclude

1. First mixture: the pepper is visible; second mixture: the table salt dissolves and forms a clear mixture.
2. Students may recall that sand and water resemble pepper and water. Accept other answers that demonstrate the same concept.
3. Students may recall that sugar and water resemble table salt and water. Accept other answers that demonstrate the same concept.

◆ Going Further

Sample experiment: Prepare two identical sugar and water solutions and two identical mixtures of sand and water; filter one sand mixture and one sugar mixture, then allow the other two to sit for a day or so. Sand will remain in the filter and quickly settle out from the mixture. Dissolved sugar will pass through the filter but will form small crystals as the water evaporates.

P9 Classifying

◆ Advance Planning

Assemble supplies. Label each piece of fabric with the name of the fabric, but not whether it is natural or synthetic.

◆ Procedure Tip

- Students may have difficulty identifying natural polymers. Point out that wool and cotton fabrics contain natural polymers.

◆ Time

15 minutes

◆ Data Collection and Observations

Individual answers will vary depending on the items in the room, articles of clothing, and fabric examples used.

◆ Analyze and Conclude

Answers will vary. Make sure students understand how to find the percent of items not made from polymers by dividing the number of nonpolymer items by the total number of items and multiplying the answer by 100%.

P10 Packaging with Polymers

◆ Advance Planning

Obtain samples of at least four different polymers used in packaging. Have a small supply of each sample available for each lab group. To save time, assign each group one of the properties to be tested.

◆ Procedure Tips

- Ask students what factors need to be taken into account when choosing a packaging material. (Strength, resistance to tearing, and cushioning) Invite them to image they are running a mail-order catalog company. Ask: What factors would your consider in selecting packaging materials for your business? (Cost, cushioning, weight, resistance to pests, effect on the environment)
- Students may want to try additional tests. Evaluate procedures for safety before allowing students to proceed.
- Guide students in controlling variables. Emphasize that only one property and one polymer should be tested at a time.
- Advise students to set up the heat insulation test first. Other tests may be performed while they wait for the time to pass until a second temperature measurement is taken.

◆ Time

45 minutes

◆ Data Collection and Observations

Students should use the results of their tests to rank the polymers according to the properties that make them suitable for packaging.

◆ Analyze and Conclude

1. Students should use their test results to compare the different materials.
2. Students should analyze each test they performed and describe how well it worked. They should suggest improvements to their procedures.

   Sample: Tyvek is water repellent and strong; it would keep the package dry. Ecofoam has good cushioning properties and is water soluble. This reduces the quantity of solid waste produced.

   Sample: Popcorn would attract insects and other animals. Plastic foam is environmentally unfriendly.
3. Answers will vary. In business, the cost of supplies must be considered. However, students may think that the advantages of these materials are worth the extra cost.

P11 Are They Steel the Same?

◆ Advance Planning

Buy the nails and bolts at a hardware store.

◆ Procedure Tips

- Cut nails have flat heads and are made of low-carbon steel; they are commonly used on hardwood floors. Wire nails are also called finishing nails.
- If possible, leave the nails and bolts in the bags for two days so students can observe more dramatic changes.

◆ Time

10 minutes, plus one- or two-day waiting period

◆ Data Collection and Observations

Students should observe that the nails rusted, but the bolt did not.

◆ Analyze and Conclude

1. Both nails rusted; the bolt did not rust or rusted very little.
2. The cut nail changed the most; the bolt changed the least.
3. The materials in the nails determine how the nails react to salt water.

P12 Does It Get Wet?

◆ Advance Planning

Purchase similarly sized glazed and unglazed flowerpots.

◆ Procedure Tips

- You may wish to lead students in a review of how to find the percent of change.
- If the pots have approximately the same initial mass, students can compare the raw data instead of the percent of change of mass. Larger pots and pots soaked longer than 10 minutes will show a more dramatic change.

◆ Time

15 minutes

◆ Data Collection and Observations

Larger pots, and pots soaked longer than 10 minutes, will show a more dramatic change.

◆ Analyze and Conclude

1. The unglazed pot gained the most mass.
2. The glazing keeps water from soaking into the pot.

P13 How Slow Can It Flow?

◆ Advance Planning

Purchase honey, plates, spoons, and tape at a food store.

◆ Procedure Tips

- Refrigerate the honey if possible.
- Students should prop up the plates using blocks or books.
- Provide damp cloths or paper towels to clean up any spilled honey.
- Write the equation for calculating speed on the board:

  Speed = Distance ÷ Time.

◆ Time

20 minutes

◆ Data Collection and Observations

Data will vary.

◆ Analyze and Conclude

1. You can tell an object is moving if it changes position over a period of time. If the object moves too slowly, you need to observe it over longer periods of time.
2. The growth of hair and the movement of the hour hand on a clock are too slow to see.

P14 Sticky Sneakers

◆ Advance Planning

Assemble the spring scales, paper clips, tape, balance, and mass sets. Bring in an assortment of sneakers or ask students to volunteer their sneakers.

◆ Procedure Tips

- Be sure students check the zero of the spring scale each time they use it. If the spring scale is calibrated in grams, students can multiply by 0.01 to obtain a reading in newtons.
- Point out that the scale must not be angled to the side or up or down while it is used, as this changes the reading.

◆ Time

45 minutes

◆ Data Collection and Observations

Students' tables should show the force of friction for each kind of sneaker.

◆ Analyze and Conclude

1. The manipulated variable is the sneaker sole. The responding variable is the amount of friction.
2. For stopping friction: the sneaker is moving at a constant speed; therefore, the friction force and the pulling force must be balanced (equal). The pulling force is indicated by the spring scale. For starting friction, the pulling force must overcome the friction force in order to make the sneaker move. At the point where the sneaker starts to move, the two forces are almost equal.
3. It is a fair test of the friction as long as the amount of friction in each sneaker depends on mass in the same way.
4. See students' diagrams. Diagrams should be clearly labeled with force arrows reflecting the size of the force and the direction.
5. You pull the sneaker at a slow speed to test stopping friction because when you stop, the sneaker is sliding slowly along the ground. You pull a sneaker that is not moving for starting friction because when you start running the sneaker is not moving yet.
6. Answers will vary. Running sneakers tend to exhibit more starting friction. Basketball sneakers tend to exert more stopping friction. Tennis shoes tend to exert more sideways-stopping friction.
7. One type of sneaker may provide better traction than another because the soles are made of a different material, they have different treads, or have worn treads or rubber soles hardened with age.
8. When you press against the floor when starting to run, you increase the force with which the sneaker and floor press against each other, increasing the friction force. To test for this variable, students could repeat the lab after adding weights to each sneaker. A suitable weight could be made by filling several resealable plastic bags with sand. These could be stuffed into the sneaker before measuring each type of friction.

P15 How Do Light Beams Behave?

◆ Advance Planning

Obtain a few polarizing filter strips from a science supply house. Cut a small section of polarizing filter (about 2 cm^2) from the strip. Shape it so that it easily fits over the lens cover on the QX3 microscope. Use a small amount of cellophane tape to hold it in place (be sure not to cover the viewing area). Assemble the supplies for the Going Further activity, if desired.

◆ Procedure Tip

- Students should work in pairs to complete this activity. They may need to observe the streams of water more than once to get the best results.

◆ Time

20 minutes

◆ Data Collection and Observations

The streams of water collide and splash into the sink. The beams of light pass through each other, with no effect on the picture. The field of view becomes black when the polarizing filters are crossed.

◆ Analyze and Conclude

This activity supports the wave model of light because the beams of light pass through each other and the water streams, which consist of particles, do not.

◆ Going Further

Polarizing microscopy is a technique used to investigate if certain substances "glow" or bend light rays twice. Select substances can be identified based on their ability to "glow" under polarized light. Salt crystals do not "glow," while sugar crystals do and appear to glow under crossed polarized light.

P16 Are You Seeing Spots?

◆ Procedure Tip

- If a color television or RGB computer monitor is not available, a VCR monitor may be used.

◆ Time

10 minutes

◆ Data Collection and Observations

Students should observe the individual colored dots that comprise the picture.

◆ Analyze and Conclude

1. The three colors are red, green, and blue.
2. Some students may realize that dots of these colors combine to form all of the other colors on the screen.